CW00815775

Dropshipping Mastery

*How to Make Money Online and Create
$10,000+/Month in Passive Income with
Ecommerce Using Shopify, Affiliate Marketing,
Blogging, SEO, and Social Media Marketing*

PUBLISHED BY: Chandler Wright

Table of Contents

Your Free Gift

As a way of saying thanks for your purchase, I wanted to offer you two free bonuses - *"**The Fastest Way to Make Money with Affiliate Marketing**"* **and** *"**Top 10 Affiliate Offers to Promote**"* cheat sheets, exclusive to the readers of this book.

To get instant access just go to:

https://theartofmastery.com/chandler-free-gift

Inside the cheat sheets, you will discover:

- The fastest way to start generating income with affiliate marketing

- My top 10 favorite affiliate offers to promote for high recurring commissions
- Access to a FREE live training where you will learn:
- how one affiliate marketer built a $500,000 a month business all while traveling the world...
- The 3-step system to eliminate risk and instability in your online business
- The 7 biggest mistakes affiliates make in making money online
- How tech companies are giving away <u>FREE MONEY</u> to help you start
- And much more...

Once again, to get instant access just go to:

https://theartofmastery.com/chandler-free-gift

Introduction

Thank you for purchasing this book.

For many decades starting a business was a very costly enterprise. It can sometimes become really complicated. You have to deal with supplies, gathering and maintaining an inventory, marketing, dealing with legalities, marketing, selling, handling customer complaints, pleasing customers, branding, and growing customer loyalty.

What if you can find a way to automate most of that?

There is a way to do that. You can do it via dropshipping. It's a business model where one man can start an online retailing store and grow it to scale along the way.

This book will explain to you the dropshipping business model from the ground up. You will also be introduced to the different concepts related to it. You will learn which sales channels are available out there and how to choose which one is for you.

You will learn how to select suppliers and wholesalers and how to deal with them. You will also learn how to spot fake suppliers too.

The guides here will also teach you how to market your store. There is a huge emphasis on this book about that. Well, after all, after setting up your store is done, the bigger and more daunting part of the work is marketing your store and selling your products.

This book also deals with growing your business after you have gotten it kick started. You will eventually grow it to a point where you can't do it on your own.

Think of this book as a guide that will give you a comprehensive and also a bird's eye view of the entire task at hand. The information here will show you the ropes. But you will have to be the one daring enough to go through the actual process.

May you find success in your endeavor and thank you for purchasing this book.

Chapter 1: What is Dropshipping

What It Is

Dropshipping is described as a retail fulfillment method and a supply chain management method. In this business model a retailer (usually an ecommerce store that has purely a web presence) does not keep any products in stock. Some dropshipping businesses have a brick and mortar store while most of them don't.

If the ecommerce store doesn't keep goods in stock the next question is how do they move products? Here's how it works. When a sale is made, the store purchases the item that was ordered by a customer from a third party provider.

This third party provider is the one that actually produces the product or at least keeps the products in stock. This third party provider can be:

- The actual manufacturer of the product
- A wholesaler
- Another retailer that actually has goods in stock

How Does It Work?

The dropshipping store places the order. Instead of putting the store's address the order will be made using the customer details of the client that actually made the order.

The third party provider then ships the goods directly to the store's customer that made the order.

There are no markings in the packaging that will indicate that the goods were shipped from the third party provider. But there are some suppliers that can arrange for the packaging to be marked with your ecommerce store's logo— but that isn't always possible.

Just like in other retail business, the store or retailer makes a profit from the difference between the original wholesale price of the product and the amount of the retail price that they charged. But that is not the only way to make money from the sale. Some product suppliers will agree to give retailers a commission based on the percentage of the sale. Again, not all suppliers or third party providers will be willing to make this deal.

Note that this business model has its pros and cons as well. You can already see the obvious benefit of not having to deal with any kind of inventory. Here are the details of the pros and cons of dropshipping:

The Pros

Let's start with the advantages of dropshipping:

1. It is easy to start

This is probably one of the biggest advantages of a dropshipping business over other ecommerce businesses.

Since you aren't dealing with any actual physical product you don't have to worry about the following things:

- You don't have to worry about managing your inventory. You don't have to keep on ordering stocks of your products.
- You won't have to bother with inbound shipments and delivery tracking.
- You won't have to handle product returns.
- No need to deal with shipping and packing.
- You cut costs because you don't have to rent warehouse space and you don't have to go through the trouble of managing said warehouse.

2. Smaller capital requirement

No warehouse or actual products to produce and manage translates to a smaller capital requirement. This is probably the biggest advantage of this business model compared to other ecommerce enterprises.

You can launch an ecommerce store without having to spend any capital for purchasing an inventory. You don't even have to produce a product.

Traditionally you had to use capital to research and develop a product to sell. The other alternative is to just sell someone else's products—which reduces your R&D costs. Either way you're still spending a good amount of money just to come up with a product to sell.

That is totally nonexistent in dropshipping.

3. Flexible Location

You can choose to have an actual brick and mortar store but that is not necessary. You're an ecommerce enterprise so a physical store just doesn't make sense but there are a few who still feel that they need to put up some physical presence.

Well, that is the case in some countries where you will be required to have some actual space before you can register your business with the authorities.

However, in most cases you won't need one. Just check with your local government authority regarding business licensing requirements and regulations before you begin your operations.

Generally, all you need is the ability to communicate with your suppliers so that you can coordinate the sale made with your customers. This means you can operate your business just about anywhere. Well, a lot of dropshipping businesses are actually run from a home office.

4. Low Overhead

With such a flexible location the next benefit that we can deduce from that is lower overhead. But there will still be expenses to be made in order to run your business.

How much on average will you have to spend each month? It will be something around $100 give or take a few.

Well, that is if you are still starting. Remember that as your business grows and scales the costs will also increase. Nevertheless, the costs will still be a lot lower compared to traditional brick and mortar retailing.

5. Lots of Products to Sell

It is easy to add and also to remove products from your online store. You don't have to do inventory and all you have to do is to watch what your suppliers put up on stock.

You can communicate with your suppliers and set things up with them so you can get the latest word on which products they have on stock. You can then put them up on your ecommerce platform as soon as these products become available.

Again, there are no additional costs that you have to cover to get this done. If a product is out of stock then you can mark it or indicate it on the product page. There are plenty of products to choose from so you have more items to offer to your clients and you can reach out to a variety of market segments.

6. Scalability

In traditional retail or sometimes in other ecommerce models, when the number of business you receive in any given period increases by 200%, then you should expect to do 200% more work than you used to. The more business you get the more time, energy, manpower, and resources you need to dedicate to fulfill orders.

That is not the case for dropshipping. You leverage the resources of your suppliers in this business model. In fact, most of the additional grunt work will be shouldered by the suppliers.

Well, you benefit from the increased orders and they also benefit from the marketing efforts that you make. So, it's a total win/win relationship. They don't have to bother with marketing and you won't have to bother with the rest of the process and focus on selling.

Dropshipping businesses can scale very well compared to brick and mortar retailing and even when you compare it to traditional online retailing as well.

The Cons

Having said all that, you should also know the downsides of dropshipping upfront. Yes it is a flexible and highly scalable model but it does have disadvantages just like other businesses.

1. Low Margin

This is the biggest downside of dropshipping so let's begin with this one. It's a very competitive industry since it is very easy to start.

Due to the increased competition a lot of dropshipping merchants and retailers tend to sell their items at rock bottom prices. That of course translates to low margins.

Unfortunately if you want to stay competitive there will be times when you have to do the same. So expect margins to be low most of the time.

Price is still king in many niches. That is true even if your competitor's website looks shoddy and if they can't even provide the least amount of customer service. Customers will look at the price points first and the rest of the details later.

2. Supplier Errors

Everything else is in your control in dropshipping, well except for the parts that the supplier provides. Your customers can blame you for something that you didn't do.

When suppliers make mistakes you have to take the brunt of the customer complaints. You just have to take responsibility for it anyway.

Case in point, you need to choose your suppliers carefully. Expect mediocre suppliers to cause you headaches quite often. The most common problems include packaging issues, damaged goods, botched shipments, and missing items.

Unfortunately even if it was not your fault this will damage your business reputation. Again, the only safeguard you have against this is to be selective of your suppliers.

3. The Shipping and Order Fulfillment Process can be Quite Complex

Again this is the part of the business that is outside of your control. Things get more complicated when you are dealing with multiple suppliers. A lot of dropshippers do that.

Computing the shipping costs to charge your customers tends to be complex if you source different products from different providers/suppliers.

Let's say a customer orders five different products from your online store. But each product is provided by different suppliers. You will have to deal with three different shipping rates.

Now, passing those rates onto the customer will make things look like you are overcharging on shipping. On top of that automating the computations will be difficult as well.

You can charge a flat rate for shipping but what about the excess cost? Who will shoulder it? You might end up paying for the excess if you do that.

The solution is to find suppliers that have almost similar shipping rates. You can just use the highest rate as your standard rate. Looking for suppliers that offer the same rates or almost the same rates will take a lot of work.

As you can see, dropshipping isn't absolutely stress-free. No business model is 100% fault-free. It also carries its own risks as well.

No enterprise is zero risk after all. However, this retail fulfillment method presents some very attractive advantages. With careful planning you can work around the potential pitfalls and solve problems proactively.

Now that you know what dropshipping is and if you think it is a very doable business then head on to the next chapter. We will go over everything you need to know about setting up this kind of business.

Chapter 2: How to Get Started with Dropshipping

Oh you made it this far. Cool! As a review of the concepts from the previous chapter, the whole dropshipping model works this way:

1. The customer purchases from your online store. You receive the payment at retail price.
2. You forward customer's order to your supplier along with the customer details. You pay for the item at a wholesale price (you make profit from the difference in price).
3. Your supplier then ships the item directly to the customer and the order will be under your name. There will be no indication that there was a 3rd party supplier since your business name will be used.

A Few Numbers to Get You Excited

The global information about the dropshipping industry is a bit limited at the moment. Everyone's still figuring things out but what we know so far is enough to spark a lot of interest.

Here are few numbers that you might want to know:

- The projected growth of global ecommerce sales is up to $4.48 trillion USD by 2021.
- The current global ecommerce sales to date amounts to $2.3 trillion.
- Manufacturers tend to profit more if their products are marketed by dropshippers by 18.33% compared to traditional brick and mortar retailers.
- In 2011, 34% of the total sales in Amazon were fulfilled by dropshippers.
- The ecommerce industry is growing at the rate of 17% each year.
- The 2017 total sales of the global dropshipping industry are estimated at $85.1 billion.
- 33% of online stores today use dropshipping as their preferred fulfillment model.

What You Need to Get Started

I hope those numbers get you really excited. If you are then you should also know that starting a dropshipping business is pretty much the same as starting a retail store. The big difference is that you just skip the part when it comes to finding storage space and creating an inventory.

You basically need the following:

- A specific niche for your dropshipping store (you may end up putting up more than one by the way).

- Choosing the right products to sell (this is related to the first bullet point)
- Finding suppliers that are reliable (this is a huge problem for beginners! So pay attention)
- Dealing with the legalities (e.g. sales tax ID etc.)
- Selecting the best suited platform for you
- Marketing your business and implementing a customer acquisition strategy (we'll spend a lot of space on this particular subject so hang on till the very end of this book).

As stated above we will spend a lot of time on implementing a strategy for acquiring customers. But since at this point we are only interested in knowing the basic stuff that you will need before you can setup a dropshipping business then let's focus on that for the meantime.

Chapter 3: How to Choose Your Niche

What is a Niche?

When we say niche we are referring to a particular market segment and not just a product or product category. For example, home audio is an entire market. It consists of a lot of different products.

A niche (i.e. a segment or small part of that market) is blue tooth speakers. Of course you can break down Bluetooth speakers into smaller sub-niches. For instance you can talk about outdoor Bluetooth speakers and there are indoor Bluetooth speakers.

What you are looking for when looking to establish a dropshipping store or site is a niche. Don't try to serve an entire market. Well actually you should narrow it down to a particular sub-niche. The more specific you are or the more narrowed down your segment is the better are your chances of making it big.

You may have heard that some people say that finding a profitable niche for dropshipping products is getting more difficult. I won't lie to you—that is true. Dropshipping has become so popular that you will find lot of niches to be quite saturated.

But that doesn't mean you won't find a profitable one. Note that new products are coming up in the markets every now and then. That creates growing opportunities for everyone. The ecommerce industry won't be growing as it is if there were no market segments that are still profitable, right?

Another claim that you may have heard is that you can be a successful dropshipping retailer in any niche. That is not true.

If you choose a particular niche that is already dominated by a lot of major brands and it is already saturated then don't expect to a lot of ROI, if any.

Well you can try. But I won't guarantee your success. In fact I would say that it will be a huge uphill battle against a favored competitor especially where a big name brand is involved.

How to Choose a Niche

Now that you know that a niche is very important to your success in dropshipping, the next question is how do you find the right ones? Here are a few factors that you should consider:

- It should be profitable (of course)
- It should have low to medium competitiveness
- It should be one that solves a real life problem (your real life problem to be exact)
- You should be knowledgeable about it

Profitability: obviously you want a niche where you can make money. So, how do you know that a niche is a profitable one? Here are a few suggestions and tools that you can use:

1. Use Google Keyword Planner

This is a free tool that you can find here:

https://ads.google.com/home/tools/keyword-planner/

You can use it to check out if there is any interest in a particular niche. You can use this tool to see how well a certain keyword (i.e. the niche you're interested in) is going to perform.

Let's say you want to test if people on the internet are looking for "Bluetooth speakers." Enter that search term in keyword planner and you will find information about it such as

- Related keywords that people are using to search for that particular product
- The search volume for each keyword (how many people are searching)
- Traffic forecasts for that search term (helps you estimate interest in the future)
- Estimated conversions (shows you how much you can potentially earn)

To access Google's keyword planner tool you need to sign into your Google Ads account (if you don't have one then you need to sign up). After that, click the Tools icon at the top of the screen.

Go to Planning and then click on Keyword Planner. Next enter the keywords that you would like to research in the box that says "Find New Keywords" and then hit enter.

You should also click on Get Started so you can access historical statistics, additional or related keyword ideas, competition data, and the number of average monthly searches for that particular keyword.

2. *Use Google Trends and Follow the Trends*

Of course you also want to know if a particular niche is still trending. It can be profitable for now but will it still be profitable 2 to 5 years from now? You don't want to jump into a dying trend or niche, right?

You need to find out if the search trend for that particular niche or search term is going upward or downward. A downward trend means that your product may not sell for long. An upward or sideward trend on the charts of course will show that there is still a lot of interest in that product/search term.

You can find Google Trends here:

https://trends.google.com/trends/

You need to enter your search term and specify a time frame. Note that you will see some graphs look like spikes, such as this one:

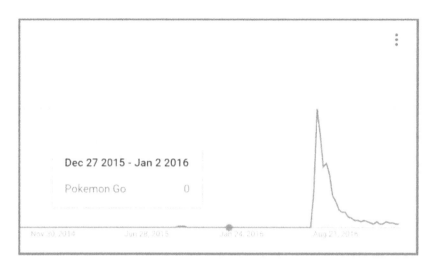

The search term for that graph is "Pokemon Go." As you can see from the graph at the end of 2015 and the very beginning 2016 a lot of people were searching for information on the internet about this game.

When things go up really high and then spike downwards quickly then that means the subject is more likely a fad. This usually happens when a new product is introduced and becomes viral or at least very popular.

Important Point: even though the graph for a certain product may spike as you can see above, it doesn't automatically mean you won't profit from that product. Remember that some products are seasonal, which is why their Google Trends graph will spike.

You can always ride the popularity and offer the product on your site when it is in season. You can also check out the news about that particular product to find out why it became popular for that season.

Some products become popular because a major brand is waging a marketing campaign on the internet. Whether a product is seasonal or something is boosting interest about it you should do your research before selecting that niche or product.

3. *Check for Products on Sale*

What better way to check if a niche is profitable than to see if your competitors are selling it? See if there are other dropshipping websites that are selling it too. You should also check out affiliate networks such as JVZoo, Clickbank, CJ.com, ShareASale, Ebay, Amazon, and others. Well, you can skip affiliate sites that focus on digital products such as Clickbank if you like.

For each product that is available in your niche, always check the number of reviews and the number of answered questions about that product. This indicates buzz that has been created about that product. Use Google Trends and Keyword Planner to confirm that buzz (and vice versa).

You should also take note of the number of products that come up when you search for it. Let's say you look for "Bluetooth speakers" on Amazon. Your results may look something like this:

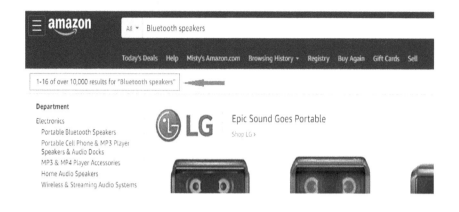

Pay attention to the number of products available with each search. If it has thousands of products then there is interest in that particular niche. In the case of Bluetooth speakers, you may have to narrow things down to a sub niche such as "portable bluetooth speakers waterproof" (**more than 2,000 results**) or "portable bluetooth speakers with wheels" (**shows 937 product results**).

That means there is a good chance that with wheels type of Bluetooth speakers will be easier to sell since there would probably be less competition for it.

GOAL: Do the same searches in other affiliate marketing sites. The goal is to confirm that there are products in your niche and to narrow down your search to a particular sub-niche where there is less competition. Simply put—*look for the underserved niche*.

Other than that you should also look for the number of merchants and retailers in an affiliate site, which is the case for Commission Junction and ShareASale.

4. Blogs, Forums, Social Media, and Message Boards

Finally, you can check out forums, blogs, social media posts, and messages boards to check if there is currently any interest in that particular product or niche. For example you can search for "no gi shorts + reddit" to see if people are still talking about no gi jiu jitsu shorts on Reddit.

Here is a screen shot of my search for that as of the writing of this book:

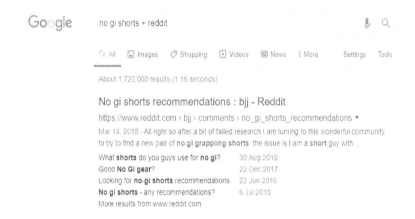

What this shows me is that there isn't much interest in it currently at least among people on Reddit. The latest post is on August 30 last year. If you check out the responses to that question they too have been posted over a year ago.

Do the same when you scope out the buzz on blogs, forums, and social media. If there is buzz about it then people are talking about it. In that case it might be a profitable niche. When on social media you should check out hashtags and group discussions.

It's not the number of likes you are looking for. Pay attention to the buzz—in other words find people who are talking about that niche. The buzz at this point is more important than likes and shares.

Research Your Competition: Check if a niche is already too saturated. If there are other competing online stores you have to decide if you are ready to compete against them. If you're just doing dropshipping for the first time then this might not be a good option for the time being.

"Scratch Your Itch" and "Fix Your Pain": this is a piece of old school advice for new entrepreneurs. If a product or products within a niche solves a personal problem that you are experiencing at the moment then that might be a good niche to investigate.

Monetize Your Passion: this is another old time entrepreneurial advice. If you are already passionate about something—maybe you are into jiu jitsu or perhaps you play guitar, then that might also be a good niche to investigate.

Remember to narrow things down since guitar playing and jiu jitsu are huge niches. You can narrow things down to classical Spanish guitars or women's no gi jiu jitsu tops.

Now that you know how to choose your niche and the other things that you need to get started with dropshipping, the next step is to find out which specific products to sell. We'll go over that in the next chapter.

Chapter 4: Choosing the Right Products

As it was stated earlier in the previous chapter, selecting the right products is related to choosing the right niche in dropshipping. Well, it's also the same thing in other ecommerce retail business for that matter.

This is actually a crucial step in this type of enterprise. You see, even if you already know the niche that you want, you may not know exactly what products to sell.

Just as we have seen in the sample searches that we have shown in the previous chapter, there could be hundreds (and sometimes even thousands) of products to choose from even in a well differentiated sub niche.

What you are looking for are not just products to sell but products that will sell. You may not have an inventory to keep in dropshipping but you are trying to save up on listing space on your site instead.

Your Audience

Here's another old time trade secret or rule of thumb that you should follow when selecting a product – you should let your target audience be the deciding factor. You're trying to sell to them and fulfill a need that they have. That is why they will proverbially decide which products you will list on your ecommerce site.

That is why one of the things that you should do is to look for customer reviews, trends, Google searches, and online chatter. The goal is to find products that people are actually interested in.

Characteristics of Products That Sell Better in Dropshipping

Is it possible to sell any product in a dropshipping business? The answer is yes. You can pretty much sell anything you can find on the internet—you can even sell toothpicks online too if you want.

However, it cannot be denied that there are certain products that will sell better in a dropshipping business and there are products that won't. Here are some of the characteristics of products that you should look out for:

- The retail price of that product should be anywhere within $15 to $200 (this is known as the sweet spot for the price of products in ecommerce)
- Products that can be sold all year round—seasonal products don't sell that well for dropshipping
- Any product that weighs less than 4 pounds is great for this business model (consider the shipping prices)

- Products that are about the size of a shoebox or those that can fit in a shoebox sell quite well (i.e. anything that is small and lightweight)
- Products that are easy to compete—that means they do not belong to a niche that is already dominated by major brands

Unsaturated and Minimal to Zero Major Brand Presence

Remember that you can't capture a good portion of the market share when you're a small business when you have a major brand dominating and saturating the market. For example, don't expect to win against Apple or Samsung by dropshipping a different brand of smartphone.

International ePacket

There is what is known as the ePacket limit—4.4 pounds. Staying within this limit prevents you from paying extra for shipping your products.

Note that the ePacket has minimum and maximum size limits. See the following table:

Minimum Requirements	Maximum Limits
Length: 14 cm (for boxes)	Length + Width + Thickness:

	90 cm (for boxes)
Width: 9 cm (for boxes)	Permissible Difference (boxes): 2 mm
Permissible difference: 2 mm (for boxes)	Maximum Length (box): 60 cm (permissible difference of 2 mm)
Length + diameter x 2 = 17 cm (minimum dimensions for rolls)	Length +Diameter x 2 = 104 cm (max dimensions for rolls)
Minimum length (for rolls): 10 cm	Maximum length (for rolls): 90 cm (with permissible difference of 2 mm)

Seasonal Products

Seasonal products are great if you already have a well-established ecommerce store. However, if you're just starting out, seasonal products will reduce your store's selling power when the products are not in season.

Potential Profit Margin

You should always consider your potential profit margin. Products that sell less than $15 have been observed to reduce your profit margin even if you sell them en masse.

However, any product that is priced over $200 is usually difficult to market especially if you want to hit volume sales.

Of course there will be a few products that will be exceptions to these rules. And you won't find a lot of those.

Products with Quality Suppliers

We will actually cover this in detail in a separate chapter. But we will just touch on this lightly just to point out how important a factor this is when selecting a product.

Even though a product looks like a good item to market (it is popular, it solves a particular need, and there is a huge demand for it) but if you can't find a good supplier for this product then it might not be a good option—for now at least.

Potential for Creating Repeat Customers

A great product should be able to create repeat business. This is actually a factor that tends to get overlooked.

What this simply means is that a good product is one that should be able to make a current customer come back to your store and buy again. That repeat business may come in the form of a part or material that needs renewing or when the actual product runs out (i.e. it is consumable).

For instance, maybe you found a Vitamin D3 supplement that sells well and has very little competition. This is a potentially good product since it can create repeat purchases from your current customers.

After they have consumed all the Vitamin D3 capsules in one box, they will need to buy another pack or box. That is an example of a repeat business.

Another example is a pocket photo printer. Sure you already sold the printer one time (and it will last for years). However, it will require ink and also a specific size of photo paper that you will also supply. Both the ink and special photo paper creates repeat business.

Fewer Breakable Parts

One of the frequent issues that dropshippers experience is shipments that get botched which end up having products getting damaged upon delivery.

You can say that the delivery of the goods is out of your control. And it is. However, if you ensure that you select a product that has fewer parts—and fewer delicate parts at that—then you are in a way reducing the likelihood of returns and negative customer feedback.

Choose products that are sturdy with few peripheral or removable parts. You can't rely on a delivery company's ability to ensure that the product will arrive at its destination in one piece.

There is also another thing you can do. You can choose a supplier that is known to provide quality packaging. Some good quality third party providers can do more than just wrap the product in bubble wrap.

Additional Tips for Selecting Products for Dropshipping

- Survey all the products in your niche
- Cross reference the potential products that you have found with the best-selling products (do a comparison)
- The products must fill a need from actual customers

Mistakes and Pitfalls to Avoid

Don't be too hard on yourself if you make mistakes especially when choosing a product to market. In fact, you may even find yourself going back to the drawing board on occasion.

We will make mistakes when we do this business and it is okay. The mistakes that we make will become our teachers—a very hard and cruel teacher at that. They will eventually help us improve.

Now, to help you avoid making major blunders, one shortcut is to learn from the mistakes that other marketers have done. Pioneers are there not only to point the way to where you should go but also to show you the pitfalls that you should avoid.

Here are some of my biggest mistakes that you should watch out for:

- **Choosing a product that is highly competitive**

Now, this I should say is a very common beginner mistake. I think every dropshipper will make this mistake one time or another.

How did that happen for me? There was a time when I thought I stumbled upon a great product—Bluetooth speakers.

I thought that it was a great product to sell online. Besides, I knew a lot about them. I owned several of those speakers myself.

I scoped the competition—I saw that there are lots of people who are selling them on eBay and also on Amazon.

I check for search words and look at that it's a hot product. There have been thousands of searches for Bluetooth speakers in the previous months and the trends show that there is a regular and steady interest in the product.

On top of that a lot of people are looking for it on social media. I noticed that there were people posting these goods on Facebook Marketplace and a lot of inquiry has been made about it at the time.

I thought the product was a winner, that maybe I could get a slice of the proverbial pie. Sure there are lots of other retailers who are already making profit from it and of course they have already grabbed a portion of the market share.

I thought that there maybe a few hundred folks out there who are looking elsewhere. And that is where I thought I could position myself.

Was it a good idea? No, it wasn't.

I have since learned that trying to squeeze my way into a highly competitive niche is a mistake waiting to happen. Sure, there is a possibility that I can grab at least a tiny portion of the market share.

But I didn't count on the price war that will happen against the competition. I was new and they were well-established. They can keep on going even with rock bottom returns but I needed the money to support a growing business.

Long story short—I ended up folding under the pressure.

- **Selling knock-offs**

I'm not saying that all Chinese made products are knock offs. It doesn't have to be made in China or some other country in the pacific. Knock offs can be produced anywhere.

Now, the thing is that you will eventually find suppliers of knock-offs and imitations. Somehow the FBI still hasn't caught them yet (or some other agency that is in charge of catching them).

Don't get me wrong. There is a market for counterfeit products. People buy that stuff. There is no doubt about it.

However, here is advice from personal experience—stay away from knock offs. It didn't happen to me but from what I learned from another colleague, you can get into some serious legal trouble if you sell those things online.

That is why you should research your suppliers carefully especially if they're new or they claim to sell the same products at very low prices.

If their offer is too good to be true then you can bet your bottom dollar that it is. Chances are they are selling counterfeits. Oh they can get away and just setup another supplier website. But if you are a beginner and you have just started a brand spanking new sole proprietorship then the legal consequences stack up against you.

Big tip: don't do it—ever.

- **Marketing a designer product**

Designer products include any kind of big name brand out there. They can also be very tempting to sell because people are always looking for them.

On top of that they are also very expensive products—which you may think could allow you to jack up your markup value. Another big piece of advice—don't try selling them either.

That's from experience as well. You think that you can increase your margin with designer products? Here's some solid truth – the profit margins for these products are very low.

They're okay for big brands and big stores because they can live with the low ROI. They have deep pockets that they can hold on to. Not you—not the dropshipper.

First off, your buying power is at stake. What if there are returns? Large retail stores can do that because frankly they have bigger funds than us smaller retailers. Unless you have that you shouldn't dabble in these products especially when you're just starting.

Best Dropshipping Products So Far

We mentioned using Google Trends in the previous chapter to help check if there is interest in a product. I have saved you the trouble of looking for some of the trending products to date.

Note that you can check these products with Google Trends and Keyword Planner to see if they are still viable for selling in dropshipping.

Here's the list:

- Kids tent

- Artificial flowers
- Calligraphy pens
- Tote bags
- Ukulele
- Sports bra
- Matcha
- Insulated bottles
- Waterproof bags
- Printed socks
- Anti-aging cream
- Seamless underwear
- Organic tea
- Smoothie blender
- Baby carrier
- Resistance bands
- Teeth whitening kits
- Muslin blankets
- Wooden watches
- Smartwatches

Chapter 5: Setting Up Your Business

In this chapter we will go over a few legalities. It should however be noted that we can't cover everything here. The laws will be different in each country. Even the laws in the North American countries of Canada and the USA are different.

That means the legal requirements for putting up your dropshipping business may be different depending on which country you're in. If you're an expat living somewhere in the tropics and you're planning to put up an ecommerce business, then you should give due diligence.

The same rule of thumb also applies to everyone—including entrepreneurs in the US. Remember that even some states may ask for a few additional requirements before you can put up an online enterprise.

Case in Point: go find a lawyer that can help you with the legal requirements. The next best option is to find another entrepreneur in your state who has already setup his or her own dropshipping business.

You can ask that person to mentor you. Well at least when it comes to the legalities.

Choosing the Most Appropriate Business Structure

The following are the most common types of businesses that are put up by dropshippers. You ought to establish your own business entity if you are truly serious about starting with this business.

- **Sole Proprietorship**: this is the simplest type of business that you can setup. It is one that is owned and managed by a single person. Think of it as a personal business that you own. In this essence, free lancers are considered as sole proprietors.

  In the eyes of the IRS (or whatever is the branch of the government is in charge of taxation in your country), a sole proprietorship is nothing different from employment. The only difference is that you earn your income from the business instead of getting it from your employer.

  You usually don't need any federal or business filings. You are only required to report your business earnings to the local government agency overseeing such business entities and you need to file your personal taxes as well.

  It's pretty simple, right? However it doesn't offer any form of protection from personal liabilities. What does that mean? It means that if someone sues your business you will also be liable for any charges or damages that have been incurred. That means your personal assets may also be placed in jeopardy if deemed necessary by the courts.

- **Partnerships**: A partnership is like a sole proprietorship but it has at least two business owners (i.e. the partners). In the USA it is defined by the US Revised Uniform Partnership Act of 1994.

  You can think of a partnership as a single proprietorship but the difference is that this one has more business owners who will share the liabilities if any. They also share in the profits since they are co-owners of the business.

  Partners file their return information together or jointly. Note that the partnership business usually doesn't pay income taxes. Each partner files this individually. Note that the partnership is not a separate entity from the business partners that formed it.

- **LLC or Limited Liability Company**: An LLC is a step higher than a sole proprietorship and also from a partnership. What this means is that your business enterprise will be considered as a separate legal entity.

  An LLC benefits from the tax freeway, which is a regulatory benefit. Think of it as a combination of the features of a corporation and a partnership. It's a great option in case you want to setup a bigger business enterprise but not big enough for incorporation.

Your business will have its own assets and in case someone files a complaint your personal belongings won't be part of any legal proceedings. In other words, the liabilities that can be incurred will be limited to the properties of the businesses only—in case someone decides to sue your company.

However, take note that this is not a foolproof protection. There are legal ways to still encroach upon your personal belongings. But at least an LLC provides you with better protection when push comes to shove.

You will be required to file additional requirements when you setup an LLC. This also means you will have to pay additional ongoing fees and maybe an incorporation fee. A limited liability partnership may have fewer fees compared to an incorporated business entity.

Note also that not all states and territories allow the establishment of LLCs. Pay attention to taxation and regulatory requirements too.

- **C Corporation**: Of the different types of business entities that have been mentioned here, this is the one that carries the most protection from liabilities. Note that a lot of the major corporations today are setup as a C Corporation.

However, do take note that setting up a C Corporation is a lot more expensive compared to the other types of businesses. They are also subject to double taxation. On top of that, the income from the company does not directly go to shareholders.

A C Corporation is also a separate entity from the entrepreneurs that set it up. Note that the ownership of the company is divided amongst its shareholders. Note that legally speaking, it is the corporation that will own the business and not the shareholders themselves but it is the shareholders who form the corporation.

Note that most dropshippers prefer to setup sole proprietorships since they are usually just run by one person. But that doesn't mean you can't partner up with another entrepreneur to get things going.

Your business might grow big in the future – it is quite possible – and thus even though you start as a solo entrepreneur you might end up finding business partners with whom you can work with.

When your business grows bigger you might also want to consider putting up an LLC if it is allowed in your state or territory. And of course if your business becomes really huge then you might look into incorporating it in the future.

What You Need to Do

At this point you just need to determine which type of business structure you want to setup. Find out the legal and regulatory requirements and then comply with them.

File your business name and also pay the necessary fees. Make sure to consult with an attorney or any expert on the subject of your local laws.

Employer Identification Number

Think of an EIN as the social security number of your business. That is what the IRS uses to identify a business entity. This should be an easy step since you can apply for one online by visiting the link below.

https://www.irs.gov/businesses/small-businesses-self-employed/apply-for-an-employer-identification-number-ein-online

Now, the thing is that not every business will be required to have an EIN. The IRS has also provided a list to help you identify if you need to apply for one:

https://www.irs.gov/businesses/small-businesses-self-employed/do-you-need-an-ein

Note that again you may have different system in your country. Some call it the tax identification number or some other term. Please check with local regulations regarding this requirement for businesses.

Getting Your Business Finances in Order

Remember that you should separate your business funds from your personal funds. When we talk about business finances that include a lot of financial matters other than the capital that you will need to start your dropshipping business.

You will also have to include funds for payment processing, registration payments, taxes, and others. Here are a few tips that will be helpful:

- ***Open a business checking account***. This will help separate your business income from your personal income. Having a separate bank account for your business will also simplify your accounting process.

- ***Open a business PayPal account***. If you plan to use PayPal as one of the payment options in your dropshipping business then it makes sense to get one for your business. Again, it's a way to simplify your accounting and separate your personal finances from your business finances. It also gives you another layer of liability protection.

- ***Business credit card.*** There are banks that offer business credit cards. It is just like your regular credit card and it can help you separate your personal from your business accounts payables. You will use this credit card to order from suppliers and also to pay for other business expenses—like the annual hosting fee for your ecommerce website.

Local Business License

In some countries you may be required to get a local business license but it may not be required in others. Again, check with the local regulatory body in your country, state, or territory to find out if you need to get a business license.

Home Office

It will be a good idea to setup your own home office. It will help you get your mind in business or work mode. You may also take advantage of some tax exemptions or tax deductions that may be available in your state or territory for having a home office.

Note that a lot of dropshippers setup home offices – you may also want to look into getting a separate phone number for your office but it isn't required.

Other Regulations

There are other regulations that will vary from country to country. They will include business regulations, customer data protection policies, anti-spam laws, trademark registrations, international ecommerce regulations, and others.

The good news is that there are guides for setting up ecommerce businesses in different countries. For example, you can find a few business setup guides provided by Shopify on their blog which you can find here:

https://www.shopify.com/blog/14926393-the-definitive-legal-guide-to-ecommerce

Note that the Shopify guide isn't comprehensive. It only has guides for some countries. You may have to look for specific information if you are operating in other countries not covered in those guides.

Chapter 6: Choosing a Sales Platform or Sales Channel

In this chapter we will start tackling how you can start getting sales. To get that done you need an actual dropshipping store to start selling products. We will go over the different sales channels or sales platforms that you can use to setup an ecommerce store.

What is a Sales Channel?

A sales channel simply put is your online store or dropshipping store. It can be a platform that you build yourself (i.e. your own website) or it can already be something that has been setup for you (a Shopify store). Sometimes it is nothing more than a seller account on a huge retailer site like Amazon or eBay.

Note that there are pros and cons to each one of these options. Now, some may think that they can just use multiple sales channels.

You can definitely do that but I wouldn't advise that you start with that. You will just end up juggling through different tasks and not being able to focus on anything. You will feel busy but you never get to accomplish anything.

Best practice dictates that you should focus on only one sales channel for now. You can try other sales platforms as you get more experience.

In this chapter we will review each option so that you can figure out which one is best for you. Note that dropshipping sales platforms aren't inherently bad. You can't say that Amazon is better than eBay.

However, you should spend some time mulling over the details of each one of them. Let's start with one of the most popular dropshipping platforms around—Amazon.

Amazon's Dropshipping Platform

When you put those two words together: dropshipping + Amazon, people have this automatic notion that this is the best option out there. Well, frankly speaking it can be. But you should also be aware of the downsides too before you jump into the bandwagon as it were. Yes, Amazon offers a huge crowd—and by huge we mean an audience that numbers in the millions. By working with Amazon you also have a global reach of actual buying customers.

On top of that Amazon has become a household name when it comes to online shopping. To millions of people around the world it is the go to place for pretty much anything you need in the house. And that has made it a hotspot for dropshippers as well.

Amazon Dropshipping Pros

1. *Your dropshipping store is exposed to a huge number of potential customers*

As stated earlier, when you work with Amazon you take advantage of the same audience that they have. Your products literally get exposed to millions of people worldwide.

This in itself is a shortcut. To capture an audience of that magnitude will take years to build. Amazon doesn't actually produce any products. It is just a marketplace where sellers like you and buyers all over the world get to meet.

When you sign up with their dropshipping program you get nothing less than a colossal sized traffic. It doesn't matter what product you want to sell. You can be sure that Amazon has a market for it.

2. *You establish trust quickly*

It is no secret that Amazon is a trusted brand. And when you do dropshipping with them you ride along with the trust that they have built with their clientele. In effect, their customers become your customers.

3. *Exclusive marketing and analytics tools*

It is no secret that Amazon has its own search engines. Apart from that they also have their own analytics and marketing tools. You are made privy to these tools which can improve your product selection, brand awareness, and of course your sales.

4. *You are given access to FBA*

Maybe one day some-time in the not so distant future you would like to venture into actual retail. But you might not want to handle the tough job of managing an inventory and shipping the products yourself.

This is where FBA comes in. FBA stands for Fulfilled by Amazon. It's a program by this retail giant where smaller retailers can ship their products to Amazon. The products will be stored in Amazon's warehouses. When a customer orders an item Amazon will ship the product.

As you can see, this is an interesting option that is afforded to you as a retailer slash dropshipper. Is it a huge perk? Well, not really but it might be something that you would like to expand your enterprise into someday especially if you are able to find a product of your own that you want to market.

Amazon Dropshipping Cons

1. *Pretty steep competition*

Remember that you're not the only dropshipper selling on Amazon. In fact, you might still find a good number of competitors even if you have narrowed down your niche.

This makes Amazon's popularity a double edged sword. On the one hand you have a high level of product exposure. On the other hand you also have lots of competitors. Sure there is a huge market there and everyone can share, right?

Well, that's not always the case. Even with a huge market sometimes the competition comes down to cut throat levels, proverbially speaking. Expect to see some price wars with competing dropshippers from time to time.

2. *Substantial listing fees*

The listing fees can also be pretty steep, which can climb anywhere from 10 to 15 percent of your product price. This high level of fees will have a direct impact on your profit margin.

If your margin is already low then these fees can be a pain in your earnings. On the flipside, even with the hefty listing fees, you are exposed to a huge audience. You will just have to try and hit volume sales at some point to make significant profits.

3. *You don't have 100% control over how your products are marketed*

Remember that it is Amazon that controls how and where your products are listed. There are options afforded to you but they don't give you the same level of freedom as you would when you do your marketing on your own website. This is one of the things you give up in exchange for lots of product exposure.

4. You can't develop the same quality of relationship with your customers

Since customers will see Amazon and not your company's actual branding then you can't expect to develop the same level of brand awareness as you would with a website of your own. On top of that there will be restrictions imposed upon you when it comes to your own brand.

5. Payment options may be a problem

Note that Amazon doesn't use PayPal as a payment option. If your customers are the type that prefers to pay through this payment channel then that can be a roadblock for you.

Another problem item that might become a problem for you is the fact that Amazon pays sellers every couple of weeks. That might mean you have to monitor your cashflow like you keep an eye on your blood pressure.

This setup may be okay for some folks but it isn't going to be a perfect fit for everybody. There are entrepreneurs who may see it as something less ideal especially if they prefer to get a hold of cash each week.

6. Exposure of sales data

It has been rumored, but I guess it hasn't been proven yet (but there have been accusations), that Amazon makes use of the sales data of merchants selling on their site.

They use this data to find out how merchants are doing, what products are selling well, and then increase their own involvement in that merchant's niche. In other words they use you to figure out what sells and then they jump in so they can make money in the same niche as well.

Again there have been allegations but nothing conclusive has been proven thus far. However it is true that Amazon will have access to your sales data—and other data as well.

You're working on their platform so you can bet that they know how well you're doing. They can also see which of your products are hot and how much money you're making off of that product.

eBay as a Dropshipping Platform

It cannot be disputed that eBay is the largest auction site in the world. They're a pioneer in that industry and so you should expect them to be the biggest one there is.

Just like Amazon, it is a website or platform that people know quite well. It has established itself as a trustworthy brand. And they have the years of experience to show for.

That is why a lot of dropshippers have also come over to eBay to market their products. However, just like Amazon, there are pros and cons to dropshipping on their platform. These two platforms have similarities however remember that eBay is an auction site so the differences will matter.

I Thought Dropshipping Wasn't Allowed on eBay?

You may have heard that dropshipping was banned on eBay. However, that isn't accurate. The truth is that you can do dropshipping on eBay.

But there are certain conditions. Here's an excerpt directly from their website:

"Dropshipping, where you fulfill orders from a wholesale supplier is allowed on eBay. Remember though, if you use dropshipping, you're still responsible for the safe delivery of the item within the time frame you stated in your listing, and the buyer's overall satisfaction with their purchase.

"However, listing an item on eBay and then purchasing the item from another retailer, or marketplace that ships directly to your customer, is not allowed on eBay..."

So, what does that policy mean?

Well, simply put, you're not supposed to get your products from another retailer or from another marketplace, like Amazon (big grin). eBay's policy is that your products must come from actual wholesalers—which is how the dropshipping business model should work in the first place.

Doesn't eBay Just Hate Amazon?

Nope, it's not about that. Yes, they are competitor market places but that is not the reason why eBay banned shipping products from Amazon. You need to hear the back story before you judge things here.

You see there was a time a few years back when dropshippers flocked to eBay using Amazon and AliExpress as their suppliers. That worked for a time.

However, it was later found out that when Amazon shipped the products to customers, naturally the item will have Amazon's packaging on it—complete with the Amazon logo.

This of course caused a lot of confusion for the customers who thought that they were buying stuff from sellers on eBay—not Amazon. But that is not the only concern that was brought up eventually.

When customers opened the Amazon branded boxes, they will also see a slip or receipts inside which will tell them that the item was provided via Amazon Prime delivery—which was actually free, if you're a Prime member.

Unfortunately, the unlucky customers who bought the items from the dropshippers on eBay charged them for the delivery, which was supposedly free of charge. Of course people felt that they were scammed and they eventually reported this malpractice to eBay.

So, What About AliExpress?

Dropshipping on eBay using AliExpress as your supplier has long been problematic since day 1. The products were shipped from China. It's not that Chinese products are all bad—well there are bad products (some are really bad and there are plenty of imitations too) but there are good quality products from China too you know.

However, the issue that was reported to eBay was that the delivery time took several weeks. Well, what would you expect? But if the customer was from Asia then the delivery would take only several days (7 days max—and that is already pushing it).

However, if you ship all the way from China heading to the US, Canada, or somewhere in Europe (or elsewhere), then expect the shipment to arrive more than a week later. This of course created a lot of angry customers.

So, what finally happened was the policy change that eBay made, part of which was quoted earlier. So, the gist of the matter is that you can dropship products on eBay but you need to source it from an actually wholesaler. On top of that you should mind your ETDs and the safety of the package.

eBay Dropshipping Pros

1. *It's easy to get started on eBay*

It's very easy to get started with dropshipping on eBay. All you need to do is to sign up for an account and then add your listing. With that you're already in business.

2. *There is less marketing involved*

Similar to Amazon, you won't need to do a lot of marketing involved when you dropship on eBay. Why? This is because the market is already there. You don't need to chase after anyone anymore just to get a sale. The people who visit the site are there to buy.

3. *Very large audience*

Just like in Amazon again, eBay also has a huge number of regular buying customers. People don't visit this site just to look around. They're actually looking to buy and the number of people who visit this ecommerce platform is in the millions.

4. *Larger margin*

Remember that eBay requires their dropshipping sellers to source their products from wholesalers. You will be purchasing items at wholesale prices and selling them at retail prices. That translates to higher margins for you.

eBay Dropshipping Cons

1. *There is no focus on the merchants*

On eBay there is very little focus on the company that is doing the selling. That means there is no increasing of brand awareness going on. There is no customer relationship being built. There are even restrictions on how you can communicate to your customers.

2. *Fewer repeat customers*

Don't expect to get a lot of repeat customers on eBay. Again, there is hardly any connection made between seller and customer. That means if a customer finds another product that they like and it is sold at a better price by a different dropshipper that is also listed on eBay then you can expect that customer to buy from your competition.

3. *You can't customize your platform*

Just like in Amazon, you have no way to customize the look and feel of things on your page. Well, for one thing it is not your site. It is not your store. You follow eBay's style guide.

4. *Listings require constant monitoring*

One of the downsides of dropshipping in eBay is the fact that you need to monitor your listing. It's not going to be like posting a static product for sale. Your list can get modified every now and then so you have to update it every now and then. There tools that you can use to automate this task but you will still have to do some grunt work.

5. *You have to pay listing fees*

Yes, just like what happens in Amazon you will have to pay certain fees to get listed on eBay. The fees can go up as high as 10% of a product's listed price (and even higher at times).

In the world dropshipping where margins are already sliced thin, fees like that can really cut into your profits. That means you have to decide whether the ROI is worth the cost of getting listed on eBay.

Dropshipping with Shopify

Shopify is one of the fastest growing dropshipping platforms today. More than 350,000 online retailers choose this platform. Basically they provide you with an ecommerce store that you can design on your own.

It is a great option for beginners since the setup process is very easy. Note that it is not the only ecommerce platforms out there. This is a true blue platform not an online retail store like Amazon or an auction site like eBay.

They set you up to create your actual dropshipping store. And then you can list products directly from your selected wholesaler. That's basically what dropshipping should be all about.

Who are Shopify's competitors? Well, here's a short list and you can also check them out as well:

- Drupal Commerce
- Symphony Commerce
- Zen Cart
- Open Cart
- Big Cartel

- YoKart
- WooCommerce
- Magneto

Again, the big advantage of Shopify over these competing ecommerce platforms is the fact that they are very beginner friendly. It's something that you might want to use if you're just starting out in dropshipping. Let's go over the pros and cons:

Shopify Dropshipping Pros

1. *Lots of available templates*

Shopify literally has tons of website templates that you can use for free. These are professionally designed themes and they are mobile ready. That means they are highly responsive—they can easily accommodate and adjust the look of your online store to the screen size of the user.

2. *Massive functionality options*

Shopify also gives you a massive amount of options in case you want to expand the functionality of your dropshipping store. They include plugins, apps, and site extensions that make your ecommerce store very useful to your customers.

They actually have more than 1,500 of these options available. Note that some of these are paid apps while others are free to use. They even allow you to connect to mobile app developers so that you can create your store's very own smartphone app.

3. Cross channel selling

You are also allowed to connect your ecommerce store to your social media page. That means you can also sell and advertise you products through social media portals like Facebook, Pinterest, Instagram, and others.

4. Built in SEO

Search engine optimization can sound very tricky—especially if you are not technically inclined. The good news is that you don't need that technical know-how if you use Shopify.

You can take advantage of the SEO tools provided with the dropshipping site. You will see all the things you need to add to each of your pages such as tags, meta descriptions, product descriptions, and others so that your page can get listed/indexed by search engines and be seen by potential leads and customers.

Shopify Dropshippig Cons

1. Selected payment options

Shopify unfortunately forces you to use their preferred payment option—Shopify Payment. That will also translate to a 2% transaction fee (cuts your margin). You can use other payment methods like PayPal or credit cards but that will mean an additional 5% transaction fee ergo you are forced to use their proprietary payment option since it is cheaper.

2. *It is not free*

There is a 14 day trial period if you want to test Shopify as a dropshipping platform. However you will have to choose one of the hosting plans that they provide after that period. The monthly charges start at $29 a month up to a whopping $2,000 monthly.

3. *CMS is limited compared to WordPress*

If you've been using WordPress to develop websites and blogs you can immediately see that Shopify kind of offers that same CMS level. However, let me warn you that it isn't the same.

Sure there are lots of options but are they the options that you would like to have? For instance, you are only allowed two types of content on Shopify's platform—product pages or blog posts. Remember that WordPress has an endless supply of plugins that can make content management easy.

4. *No options for scalability*

Just like the issues with Amazon and eBay, you are also sort of stuck with Shopify if you start to scale your business—maybe after a year of solid growth you want to move your business to a bigger platform.

You will basically lose all the rankings and authority that your online store has gained once you move out of Shopify's hosting. It will also be a pain if you try to move all your content out of Shopify as well.

In essence, it will be like starting all over again from scratch. Well, you can export your data, that's for sure. But it will be a lot of hard work not only from rebuilding your site but also when it comes to rebuilding your online store's reputation and authority.

Dropshipping With Your Very Own Store

All of the options that we have covered here thus far are third party providers that will host a dropshipping store. This last option is one that you host on your own. The big downside—I should warn you beforehand—is that you will be working from the ground up.

You won't have the advantage of having millions upon millions of regular customers. You won't have a lot of ready-made tools that you can use to setup your store. The payoff on the other hand is that you get total freedom on how you want your dropshipping store to be like.

You will have 100% control over your own branding. You will have total control over your content. Well, this is a website that is totally your own. That level of freedom does come at a cost.

Pros of Dropshipping on Your Own

1. *100% branding control*

You have complete control over all the details of your dropshipping store. You get to dictate which payment options you would like to use. You get to choose the theme. All the content is yours and you get to decide which products get displayed first.

2. *No third party fees*

The only fees that you will have to worry about will pertain to your website's maintenance. That includes hosting fees, payments for plugins and tools that you install, and other features that you would like to add to your online store.

The other fees of course include the ones charged by your wholesaler—but that is a separate matter of course.

3. *This is a real business that is completely your own*

Sure you will be in business with Amazon, Shopify, eBay and other third party hosting providers. But in reality you are at least partially working for them. That is the case when you setup your dropshipping store with these business entities.

An independent website is something that something that you can build and grow. It can also give you a sense of fulfillment in the long run.

Cons of Dropshipping on Your Own

1. Expect less traffic when you start your dropshipping store from scratch. You will have to work hard to market your store online. You will have to use SEO and paid advertising to get the word out.

2. Things can also get complex every now and then since you're still figuring things out. What do you do when your site experiences some downtime? What do you do if a page doesn't load properly? Remember that you are your own tech support in such situations. Well, you can outsource the tech issues but you still need to know what's going on.

Chapter 7: Branding Your Dropshipping Business

What is Branding Anyway?

This is an important part of establishing your business when you are just new to dropshipping. You can say that branding is the way people will identify your ecommerce store. It's your store's identity—simply put.

Some experts say that branding includes anything that will help customers and potential leads to recognize your business. In fact it also reflects how they experience your business.

It is a blanket term that envelops the presentation of your business and what it stands for. You show your brand in the way you advertise, the marketing materials you use, how your office looks like, your business cards, your employee uniforms (if you happen to expand to that in the future), and it is even displayed through your style of customer service.

Jeff Bezos, the founder of Amazon.com once said that:

"Your brand is what other people say about you when you're not in the room."

What did he mean by that? What it means is that your brand is the representation of your business reputation.

Your brand will also set your business apart from the competition. You can say that it is the overall personality of your business. Your brand reflects the strengths of your business along with its other intrinsic qualities.

Having said that, remember that when you create your brand you should do a good amount of in depth market research. A good brand will help make your business more memorable.

Combined with quality products and services, your brand will help to build relationships of trust with your customers. Customer confidence increases because of these positive experiences.

You increase trust and customer loyalty because of these things. It will happen in spite of negative customer experiences that may occur from time to time. There is a magic ratio that you should keep in mind to maintain this trusting relationship between customer and seller.

Are you ready for it? There should be at least 5 positive experiences to every single negative experience that a customer has with your store. One way to create that positive experience is through branding.

It has been observed that launching a business with a strong brand improves your chances of success.

Types of Business Brands

Branding should be part of your overall business planning regime. Note that different types of brands will suit different types of products. Since you will eventually set up more than one dropshipping store, you will have to consider branding each one differently.

The following are the different types of brands that you may consider when creating a branding scheme for an ecommerce store that you will put up.

Attitude Branding

Attitude brands are based on the physical characteristics of the product that you want to sell on your dropshipping site. If you want to sell sports products for instance, then you want an attitude brand that sends messages like power, energy, and even freedom.

Functional Branding

Functional branding focuses on the reasons why people should buy from your business. They will usually emphasize the physical characteristics and the features of your products than create an emotional connection with customers.

Functionality can be anything from better performance compared to the competition, better prices, or unique products. Other benefits of your products can also be highlighted using functional branding.

Symbolic Branding

Symbolic branding has similar traits to attitude branding. You can also say that it is the opposite of functional branding to some degree. You usually use this type of branding if you want to emphasize the emotional aspects of your business.

It can be used to show to clients that they can trust your business. It can also convey a sense of security. This is the type of branding scheme that you will want to use for service businesses. The goal behind symbolic branding is customer retention.

Individual Branding

This is the type of branding that you want to use in case you want to give each product you sell a kind of persona. You also have the option to create a separate brand for each product in your store.

This is sometimes the case when you have several products in your dropshipping store that belong to the same category. Let's say you have Bluetooth speakers and there are different types of these speakers listed on your site.

You can create an individual image or theme for each Bluetooth speaker in your list. This is actually a tactic of large corporations too. They introduce two competing products and create different brands even though they own both.

Why would they want to do this? It actually works since it creates opportunities for them to grab a larger slice of the market share. In short, think of it as a net. If customers don't get caught in one brand (the proverbial net) then they can get caught in the other net (the competing brand that they also own).

Private Labels

Private labels are also known as store brands. This is the branding scheme that you will want to use if you want to put your online store's name in the frontline. This is actually the same branding strategy used by supermarkets.

Here's an example, let's say you want to sell a cosmetic line—let's say lipstick crayons. You can launch a section of your dropshipping store that is dedicated to this brand of product. You can call it the "perky line" of lipsticks and the design of the page can even match the design and color of the lipstick crayons that you want to sell.

Know Your Audience: The First Step

Believe it or not, the first step in building your brand is to define your target market or your audience. This should also be one of the first things you should do when you put up any business.

Define the market segment that you want to serve. After defining the general market segment—upper class market, middle class, budget level/thrift etc.—you should then delimit or narrow down your segment even further.

Be as specific as you can. Here are a few examples:

- Exchange students from abroad
- Executives who recruit professionals
- Tech savvy seniors
- Work from home single moms

You should also define certain demographics such as level of education, income level, location (urban or countryside/tropics or wintery locations etc.), gender, and age group.

Internal Branding

Your internal branding will define how your business will impact your targeted market segment. What is internal branding?

Internal branding is something that some solo dropshippers tend to overlook. Sometimes it may look insignificant but if you pay attention to it, this can be a driving force that will push your business forward through rough times.

Internal branding refers to the inner values that your business stands for. If you're a sole proprietorship then you should still go back to this brand to help get your bearings straight as it were.

Imagine a tough time when orders are dwindling and customers are complaining due to botched deliveries. What do you do?

You first go back to your internal branding—what is stated in your company's core values? What do they say? They might say something like customer service first profit second—or something like that.

Now you review what went wrong. Your current supplier isn't big on customer service. That means they don't align with your company values. Then what do you do? You switch to a different supplier—one that has values the same as yours.

Create a Mission Statement

There are those who think of mission statements as corny. Some even think they are futile and useless. However, to those who have made use of them they have laid the foundation for a company's point of view.

A company without values except for profit making will miss profit making. That might sound superficial but if you take some time to mull it over you will see the value of being value driven.

If your only focus is to create more profit then it will show up in the way you operate your business. You will always want to create profit first and it will show in your policy making, in the decisions that you make, in your product selection, and in your interaction with your customers.

However, if you put providing value first then you will be surprised to find that profit tends to follow and flow in naturally. Customers will notice that you're after every buck in the way you do customer service and the way you formulate your deals.

And that is why providing value to customers should first be a priority especially when you formulate your mission statements.

So, what is a mission statement?

A mission statement is an action oriented statement that describes the purpose of a business as it serves its target market. It is a declaration of the purpose you want your company or dropshipping business to achieve.

At the founding of Microsoft, their mission statement was:

"A computer on every desk and in every home"

Now, looking back it looks like they have helped to achieve that ideal to a great degree. They may not have provided every home with a desktop computer but they revolutionized the presence of computers.

Now, Ikea has the following mission statement:

"To create a better everyday life for the many people"

Note that there is always an action to be done in that statement. So when formulating yours, create an action that you want your company or dropshipping business to perform.

TED on the other hand has the following mission statement:

"Spread ideas"

As you can see, you don't have to make your mission statement a long piece of text. Keep it concise and most of all keep it value driven. A lot of the really successful companies today have value driven mission statements.

Mission Statement vs. Vision Statement

Now other than a mission statement you will also want to create a vision statement. A vision statement is something that will tell you what your company wants to aspire to become.

You call it a vision statement because you want to reflect what you want the business to be in the future after it has achieved its mission. And more importantly, you should also include what the world will be like due to the success that your company has achieved.

You can think of a vision statement as the statement of goals and objectives that your company aspires to. A vision statement is the "what" of your company in the future while the mission statement is more of the "how" it will achieve that vision.

For example, the vision state of the Alzheimer's Association goes like this:

"A world without Alzheimer's disease"

Notice that that statement doesn't tell you exactly how their organization is to bring about the end of the occurrence of Alzheimer's disease. It is just a declaration of the ideal that the company wants to achieve.

Think of a vision statement as the objective that you want your company to achieve while the mission statement as the overarching strategy that you will use to achieve it (which includes the various tactics that you will employ).

What You Should Do

Both vision and mission statements help build your brand internally. Building your brand should be an inside-out experience. Draft at least 10 mission and vision statements.

It doesn't have to sound perfect but don't make it sound corny either. It should be down to earth and it should reflect the value that you want to give to your customers.

Next, narrow down your statements to the best 3 that you have on your list. Dwell on those three. Think about it overnight. Try to see which ones truly reflect your character as an entrepreneur.

From the final three on your list, look at the statements as if you were the customer of your business. With that point of view, which one helps to identify what benefit your business gives to you as a customer?

Answer that question and you have it made.

Now, you should also note that you will need to change your mission and vision statements as your company grows. That means you will have to go through this same process again a few months to a year from now. You will have to evaluate if your current mission and vision statements still falls or aligns with the direction your company is going.

Differentiate Your Brand

You should research what the big brands are doing as well. You're not there to imitate what the competition is doing. What you want to do is to avoid copying what they do but at least you should know what they are doing well.

Maybe you can pick up a few tips and tricks along the way. You should also pay attention to where they fail. Is there a market segment that they are neglecting? Which of their products aren't selling that well? Why?

Your goal here is to make your brand stand out. If not people will think that you are just another knock off of that big name brand.

Try to answer the following questions:

- Do they market online and offline?
- How many social mentions do they get?
- How many customer reviews do their products have?
- What is the quality of their products and services?
- Are they consistent when it comes to visual identity and messaging? Where do they tweak things a bit?

External Branding/How to Build Your Brand

Now that you have completed your internal branding, your next step is to build your brand or to do what is called external branding. This is where you get to express your internal brand to the world around you—particularly the market segment that you want to serve.

The focus of brand building is to create awareness of your business and the value that you can give. To do that you will need to employ a variety of marketing campaigns that align with your overall strategy.

Remember that the ultimate goal in branding is to create a differentiated and unique company image that will be easily recognizable in a vast and crowded marketplace.

Which Strategies Work in 2020 and Beyond?

There are a variety of strategies that you can employ that will work in the coming year and beyond. You will need a well-designed website, consistent messaging, a strong visual brand, good public relations, customer satisfaction, and a variety of advertising strategies.

A lot of these topics will be covered in the next chapters. But we will only go over some of them here.

So, which strategies do you think you should use to build your brand? Here are a few suggestions:

- Logo Design
- Improved customer experience (i.e. the performance of your website)
- Copywriting
- Search Engine Optimization
- Social media marketing
- PPC or paid advertising
- Email marketing

Some of the topics above such as SEO, social media marketing, and others are covered in other chapters. We will just go over some of the strategies above that are not covered there.

Logo Design

Logos are very powerful tools simply because human beings are visual creatures. It is almost instinctive for someone to see a logo and be reminded of their experience about the company that owns it.

Pitfall: one of the worst things that you can do is to make your logo look too generic. It is like a sign or logo that everyone has seen before and thus forget easily. You want something that people will strike a chord in people and solicit an emotional response. Remember that people remember things better when they associate an emotion with it.

Logo Design Tips

1. *Know Your Brand*

This is where your mission and vision statements come into play. You don't want to create a brand that doesn't align or agree with what is stated there.

What sort of brand are you promoting? Is it a tough brand or is it a soft brand?

What message are you trying to covey? Are you trying to spread peace, love, and unity? Or is that you are pushing strength, power, and independence?

You will pick your logo elements taking these factors into consideration. That includes the lines, colors, symbols, shapes, and other elements.

2. *Create a Strong Emotional Impression*

What colors and shapes give your logo a strong impression about your business? If your business is all about fast delivery then does the font used on your logo look like it depicts speed or does it look like a slow moving object?

3. *A Play on the Colors*

Colors convey a distinct message. Bright colors convey energy, aggressiveness, and passion. Darker colors reflect authority and mastery. Different colors also impress different emotions. For instance, the color blue can evoke feelings of unity and intelligence.

4. *Choose Your Fonts Carefully*

The typeface of your font conveys the personality of your brand. For example, toy companies usually use fonts that look like they were handmade or handwritten. This conveys a child-friendly message in the eyes of customers.

Sports brands use solid fonts. Bands use fonts that match their music—swirling script like fonts for party and 70s groove bands, sharp contrasting and aggressive looking fonts for rock and heavy metal (think of Metallica's lighting shaped font), etc.

Don't mismatch the fonts with the brand. This will cause mixed messages sent to customers and will make your brand easier to forget.

5. *Logotype*

Some companies like to use symbols for their logos. The symbol of course is the trigger that you want customer to think about you. For instance, Apple of course uses an apple as their logotype but its signature is the bite (or byte to be exact) on the side of the apple.

6. *Keep It Simple*

In today's world of mobile phones and smaller screens you don't want your logo to be too complex that it looks awkward on these devices. The simpler the logo design the better it is in today's world.

That means you shouldn't use a cacophony of colors, fonts, shapes, and symbols. Choose 1 to 3 colors, a shorter brand acronym, simpler fonts, and only one logotype, shape, or symbol.

7. *Scalable*

You want your logo to be scalable. For example, Apple used to have a very complex logo—Isaac Newton sitting next to an apple tree. It was then replaced by the rainbow colored apple. It stayed with the company for more than 2 decades.

It was finally replaced by Steve Jobs into the monochromatic design that we are familiar with today. Now their logo is easy to spot whether it's on a billboard or on your phone's screen.

8. *It Should Still Look Good in Black and White*

Not all prints can be in color. Sometimes depending on the theme of a poster, billboard, and maybe a page on a magazine, your logo should still look good and recognizable. That means it shouldn't be color dependent. It should look good with color and also in black and white.

Hiring a Freelance Logo Designer

Freelance designers can give you more bang for your buck especially if you're starting small. A design firm may charge you too much for a logo. If you don't have any design skills then you're stuck. Good thing there are freelance designers that you can hire for a reasonable fee.

Online marketplaces like Fiverr, Upwork, Dribbble, and 99Designs have hundreds of logo designers who have entire portfolios of labels that you can choose from. The only downside here is that you should watch out for generic logos that look vaguely familiar.

When you hire someone to design your logo for you, you should give him/her your style guide. This includes:

- Web elements you have on your site

- Image style
- Photography you prefer to have
- Iconography
- Preferred fonts and topography
- Color palette
- Preferred logo size
- Logo placement

You may also want to add a tag line or a slogan to your logo. It should be a short statement that expresses what your brand is all about. You can use this tag line as a marketing tool as well.

Select a Brand Voice

Your brand voice will depend on the market segment you are serving as well as on your mission and vision statements. For example, if your target segment is stay at home moms then you want a brand voice that is relatable, friendly, and personal. If you're serving professionals and executives you want a brand voice that is authoritative and professional.

Here are examples of brand voices:

- Informative
- Conversational
- Promotional
- Technical
- Authoritative

- Service oriented
- Friendly
- Professional

Website Design

Another important tool for external branding is your actual website. It's not only a sales channel; it's also your branding vehicle. However, do take note that if you choose Amazon, eBay, etc. then there's nothing much you can do about the design of your website.

But if you opted for using your own website (maybe you chose Shopify and others) then you have some form of freedom when it comes to branding your business on the web.

Why not just use a generic theme?

You may have seen hundreds of websites use the same WordPress or Squarespace theme. Was there anything that made them standout? The truth is there's nothing really that make people remember your site when you use a generic theme.

You should set aside a reasonable budget for your web design. You don't have to do it yourself and this subject is as complex as dropshipping. You can write an entire book on web design too if you like.

However, if you have up to date tech skills then you should outsource your web design. Again, if you're just starting out then you can hire a freelancer who will do it for you for a reasonable fee—don't short sell your designer though.

If your site has grown and you have made quite a profit then you can hire an agency to redesign your website. Here are just two reminders about branding and web design:

- Integrate your brand into the design of your website
- Make your dropshipping site unique
- Use it to create ongoing sales and repeat customers
- Make it optimal and user friendly
- Don't use a complex menu system

Web Design Pitfalls

Now, whether you hire someone to design your site for you or if you want to design it yourself, there are pitfalls that you should avoid. Here they are:

- ***No clear call to action*** – your website should invite the user to go to a certain page, add items to their cart, proceed to check out and buy something, contact you, or maybe do something else on the site (sign up for a newsletter/product catalog, download a free buyer's guide, enter their email address etc.).
- ***Not using analytics tools*** – we will cover analytics tools on chapter 9 of this book. Analytics

tools can help you find out what parts of your marketing strategy is working and which products tend to sell better. You also get a clearer picture as to who your customers are using these tools. Not having them on your dropshipping store is a big mistake. More on that later.

- *Unclear brand message* – this goes back to the principles that we have covered earlier in this chapter.

- *Weak SEO* – you want a lot of people finding your site organically. That means they discovered your dropshipping site by searching it on Google or some other search engine. We'll also cover SEO in the next few chapters.

- *Contact info is hard to find* – customers might want to call you or at least send you an email to inquire about your products and other transaction details. Not having a contact page will become a frustration to customers and will lead to a negative experience.

- *Slow load times* – you lose site visitors if your page loads slowly. The idea is for each page to load in 3 seconds or less. Slow load times also affect your SEO and site rankings.

- *Not designed for mobile* – the majority of internet users today use their phones and mobile devices to check out websites. Make sure that your site is responsive, which means it can adjust the page depending on the visitor's screen size.

The other branding and marketing tools and strategies mentioned earlier will be discussed in a separate chapter of this book. In the next chapter we will go over the details on finding and working with suppliers.

Chapter 8: Finding a Supplier and Working with Them

Finding a reliable supplier is one of the biggest stumbling blocks for every dropshipper. That is why this is one of the most important things that you need to decide on.

You may be a great marketer but if your supplier screws up then you end up trying to fix things. And a lot of times the causes of these troubles were outside your control in the first place.

You should take every precaution to find the right suppliers. There are several strategies that you can use. With some practice you will learn to spot a reliable wholesaler and avoid the bad ones.

The Makings of a Good Dropshipping Supplier

The following are the characteristics of a great dropshipping supplier:

1. The Absence of Huge Per-Order Fees

Wholesalers and suppliers will usually charge what is called a per-order fee. This is a fee that covers for the time and resources necessary to get your order packed and shipped to your customers.

Some suppliers take advantage of this and will charge a rather high fee. So, how much of a fee are we looking at? It usually ranges anywhere from $2 to $10 (and sometimes higher).

You should factor that when you select products since this fee will be added to the actual product price that you need to display on your ecommerce site.

Sometimes the fee can get too high and you end up reducing your profit margin. Remember that $10 might not sound much but if your competitor can lower their prices by $5 because their supplier charges them less then you can bet customers will choose to do business with them instead.

2. Quality Products

Here's a rule of thumb. If you provide quality products then you should expect lower product return orders from your customers. It also translates to the following:

- Better product reviews, which in turn boosts sales
- Fewer returns
- More organic and word of mouth referrals
- Higher rate of customer satisfaction

Are there any downsides to finding a supplier that can provide you with quality products? Well, I can think of only one—possibly lower margins.

That means you can't jack up the prices of your products a lot higher. However, even if you don't make a huge amount of profit per product sale, you will end up getting more profit from volume sales.

The more satisfied customers you have the more potential repeat orders you will get. That can also translate to more profits from referrals and the increased number of customers.

Yes, you may get low margin per sale. But that is a lot better than getting high margin sales but low quality products. It will not benefit you in the long run.

3. They Give You Access to Big Name Brands

Earlier it was mentioned that you should avoid big brand products. Yes it is true. But that is a rule for beginners— hope that clarifies things. After your dropshipping business becomes a big hit you might want to look into selling big brand products.

Brand name products also represent better quality products. A good and reliable wholesaler is one that can supply you these products. If big name brands trust them then you can trust them as well.

4. Helpful Representatives and Years of Experience

Of course it goes without saying that you should look for a supplier who has been doing it for a while. Their years of experience sending products to customers will be a big thing to lean on especially when untoward incidents happen.

That means if there is a botched delivery (e.g. damaged goods upon delivery, wrong delivery, missing items etc.) then you can coordinate with the supplier to amend the situation.

No one is perfect—we should all know that by now. And even the best suppliers and wholesalers who employ the highest standards will make mistakes from time to time.

Remember that these businesses manage hundreds if not thousands of orders every single day. Mistakes and blunders will happen every time that happens. You can chalk it up to Murphy's Law I guess.

If there is one thing that can make up for that is rep from the supplier that you can talk to that can answer all your questions. Of course, you can't expect them to know all the answers but the really good reps would be more than willing to find out what happened to an order and get back to you.

They will know how to handle any issues that come along. They will also be able to answer any questions that you might have. And if they don't have an answer at that moment they will go out of their way to find out and give you an update.

5. Fast Shipping

Delays will always make customers unhappy—and obviously you don't want that in your dropshipping business. If your supplier can't deliver the goods in 24 hours then they are not good for this kind of enterprise.

But you can give them a 24 to 48 hour window to get the goods delivered. However, do take note that a48 hour delivery window is pushing it.

Dropshipping is a very competitive business. There is no room here for delayed shipments. If your ecommerce store is known for delays then your competition will eat you alive.

However, if you do find a wholesaler or a supplier that delivers things on time every time, then you have just found a goldmine. You already have a competitive edge.

Customers will like that a lot. Now, you can test your supplier by creating a test order. Order something yourself and have it shipped to you.

That way you get first-hand experience at how fast the supplier gets the order delivered. And you also get to see the quality of their service. You can do this to test two different suppliers or wholesalers. The one that can get things done in record time should be the winner.

6. Technologically Invested

You're going to be running a store that will be cloud based. That means you need to partner with someone or another business that is also just as committed to technology as you are.

Your supplier should be one that also takes advantage of the latest technologies. That means that both of you should be on the same page when it comes to automation, scalability, and of course efficiency.

This will be increasingly important as your dropshipping enterprise grows and of course along with that comes an increase in the number of orders. The more customers you serve the more difficult it will be to manage these orders if your supplier is still doing things manually or on paper.

Remember that you may not be the only dropshipper that your wholesaler is serving. If it is a good wholesaler then chances are that other dropshippers will also take advantage of their services as well.

Now, how do you know if a wholesaler or supplier is also invested in today's technology? They should have at least the following:

- They have automated order placement and order cancellation.
- There are also options to place and also cancel orders via email
- Their product listings are updated as fast as their inventory listings
- The products on their website have updated and detailed information.

Note that not all suppliers will have all of that information readily available on their website. But if there is a number that you can call and the support staff can answer all of your questions then you might be looking at a good provider— their tech needs to catch up but they'll get there one day.

Note also that you shouldn't also judge a supplier based on how good looking their site is – if there is a secondary method to get you the info that you need then they're good to go.

7. Dedicated Support Reps

The sales rep that answered your call or product inquiry shouldn't be the same person you talk to if something goes wrong with your order. In fact the really good supplier can assign a representative to you to help monitor your situation until it is resolved.

8. Order by Email or by Phone

This is a small thing but this can actually go a long way. There should be alternative ways to place an order. What if the supplier's website experiences a downtime and you have lots of orders?

If a supplier can accommodate other methods of placing and managing orders then you immediately solve a problem right there. At least you know that this wholesaler or supplier can manage and fulfill orders during difficult situations.

How to Find a Great Supplier

Again, the goal is to find a supplier or wholesaler that is reliable and also legit for that matter. One of the simplest ways to find a good dropshipping supplier is to do a Google search.

The easiest way to find a supplier is of course through Google. You just need to open your browser and use the following search term:

<name of product> + dropshipping supplier + <country or location>

Here's a sample search term I used:

socks dropshipping suppliers Australia

And that pulled up over a million results. I didn't know it would pull up that many search results. But if you look closely the SERPs provided by our favorite search engine really didn't give me purely a list of supplier websites.

Some of the websites listed on the first few pages weren't even in Australia. Some were lists of wholesale sock manufacturers in China, UK, and the US. I guess these manufacturers also ship to Australia, which is why they're on the top of the list—not sure though.

Of course with that many on the list it will be like looking for a needle in a haystack, right?

Attend a Trade Show

Trade shows don't happen a lot but when one does you should make the effort to attend it. This way you can find out who the manufacturer is. You can even come up to a rep or the manager and ask for information yourself.

Find the suppliers and manufacturers that provide the products you are interested in. You can ask for their contact info and introduce yourself as retailer interested in their products. You can then ask them questions like payment terms, warranties, and others (more about that later).

Order from the Competition

This is a good trick that you can do if you know that a competing ecommerce store is actually dropshipping their products. Here's how you do it.

Make a small order of the product that you are interested in. When the product arrives check out the return address. Look it up on Google and see which business is on that property.

Sometimes it works and sometimes it doesn't. This at least gives you an idea who the original shipper is—which may likely be the wholesaler or the manufacturer. The next step is to get that company's contact information.

Look for Dropshipping Supplier Directories

So, doing a Google search can give you an idea but you will have to fine tune your search. You need to use something better. So, what is better than organic Google searches?

You need to search for supplier directory sites. Using supplier directory sites is a kind of shortcut since the people behind these sites have done the background research for you. Here are some of the benefits that you can get from using them:

- **Faster research** – you can quickly find out the product offerings of each supplier. Some suppliers are listed by product type. Their contact information is already given.
- **Easier searches** – you can easily filter out the search by different category. You can filter the results by product, price range, and other specs that you need.
- **Lowers your risk** – the list provider has done the grunt work and has taken out the scammers.

List of Popular Suppliers

We have a list of the most popular suppliers below. The information about each of these suppliers can help you decide which one to choose for each particular product. Note that there are pros and cons to using their services.

Since they are popular and highly rated then you can be sure that they offer the best delivery and also have some of the best products. However, since they are popular you should know that you're not the only dropshipper that will take advantage of their services.

That means that there will be times when these guys will be overloaded with orders that they might have trouble keeping up. Some of the businesses in the list below aren't necessarily wholesalers. Some of them are online directories that will point you to actual suppliers.

1. AliExpress

This is one of the most popular dropshipping platforms and also a wholesaler. They also help connect dropshippers like you to actual suppliers. Take note that a lot of their suppliers are from China.

However, take note that their suppliers are a mix—some are good and some are not so good. If you want to make sure then run a test order.

The good news is that they have suppliers from more than 40 niche categories—which is a lot. You can find pretty much everything from apparel to electronics. The other good news about them is that they have free sign up.

2. Doba

This is actually a marketplace where manufacturers and suppliers are listed. You can search for suppliers and manufacturers by product or industry. They have done the research for you so can find good suppliers for your selected product. The downside is that their service comes with a monthly fee of $29 (minimum).

3. Worldwide Brands

This is a massive directory of bulk distributors and wholesalers. Their list of suppliers covers pretty much every niche you can think of. The best part is that they make sure that each company on their list is reliable and reputable. The downside is that there is a huge one-time fee to sign up with them amounting to $249.

4. Dropship Direct

This is a general supplier and they offer more than 100,000 products on their list. The products are all shipped from their warehouses. Other than a huge product list and an expansive warehouse system they also offer you data on the different products such as the number of orders, cancel rates, etc. on each product.

They provide you with a lot of metrics that will help you decide if a product will sell well or not. On top of that, they have free sign up.

5. Mega Goods

If you're interested in selling electronics then this is the supplier that you might want to check out. Their products include Bluetooth devices, TVs, kitchen appliances, cameras, clocks, and others. They charge a service fee of $14.99 per month.

6. National Dropshippers

This is a wholesaler that has more than 250,000 products in their warehouses. Since they are a huge warehousing company they can offer products at 50% MSRP, which can potentially increase your margin per sale.

The downside is that they have monthly service fee of $19.99 and they charge you $2.49 for each order they serve.

7. Dropshipper.com

This is a dropshipper platform and they connect you to more than 890 suppliers. They have a massive product listing of almost 2 million types of products. They have everything from electronics to beauty products.

They charge a one-time fee of $99. It's either that or you pay a monthly fee of $69.

8. Inventory Source

This is actually a dropshipping network that can connect you to more than 150 suppliers. They also connect you to dropshipping platforms such as Amazon, eBay, Shopify, BigCommerce, and the like. Their service plans start at $50 a month.

9. Sunrise Wholesale

This is actually a wholesaler that offers more than 15,000 types of products. Their product categories include garden decorations, jewelry, sports and fitness, home decors, and lots more. They also connect you to dropshipping platforms like Amazon, eBay, and Shopify among others. They require a membership fee of $39.95 per month or $99 each year.

10. Wholesale Central

This is another wholesaler or supplier directory. And the good news is that it is free to access. You can search their directly using different filters. You can also search by product niche such as pet supplies, candles, books, and eye wear among others.

11. Wholesale2B

Wholesale2B connects you to suppliers that provide more than a million types of products. They connect you to more than 100 suppliers and connect you to dropshipping platforms such as Amazon, eBay, Shopify, and BigCommerce among others. Note that service fees vary depending on the platform you want to connect to.

12. SaleHoo

This is a wholesaler and supplier directory. They give you access to more than a million products from a lot of suppliers. You get to choose from more than 40 niche categories. They require an annual fee of $67 and they give you a 60 day money back guarantee.

13. Trendsgal

This is actually a global seller. They also supply kids clothes, shoes, jewelry, and other forms of clothing.

14. Nordstrom

This used to be an online store but now they also have a dropshipping program where you can offer their products on your own dropshipping website. If you're interested in marketing their brands then visit their dropshipping program page by going to https://shop.nordstrom.com/c/drop-ship-program

15. Modalyst

This is another clothing provider that also has its own dropshipping program. Their clothing line range from low cost goods to high quality designer items—that means you have a big range to work with. They offer a free forever plan that allows you to place an unlimited amount of orders.

16. Clothing Showroom

This is another clothing wholesaler. They offer pretty much everything in their clothing line and they also sell plus sizes as well.

17. CCWholesaleClothing

This is a Los Angeles based women's clothing wholesaler. Their product line covers more than 3,500 items and new items are added each week.

18. Collective Fab

This is a fashion and beauty provider that offers more than 6,500 products to choose from. Their dropshipping services come with a fee of $29 each month.

19. Born Pretty

If you're interested in marketing beauty products, cosmetics, jewelry, make up, nail art, nail polish, and others, then you should consider them as specialists in this niche. Their dropshipping services are free but you have to sign up for their webstore program.

20. Brands Gateway

This wholesaler is based in Sweden and they provide worldwide shipping. Their product categories focus on jewelry, shoes, clothes, and accessories. They also have brand name products such as Armani, Versace, Dolce & Gabbana, and others.

21. Collective Fab

As the name implies this supplier focuses on products in the fashion and beauty niche. They offer more than 6,500 types of products. They require a monthly fee of $29.

22. Rubyimports.net

This is a wholesaler that specializes in jewelry. They are based off Memphis, TN.

23. Richard Cannon Jewelry

This is another jewelry supplier. They are actually a leading manufacturer as well. They're basically a jewelry manufacturer with a dropshipping program. You may want to check them out when you decide that you're ready for selling brand name jewelry.

24. Plum Island Silver

As you might have guessed, this manufacturer specializes in sterling silver jewelry. They have a dropshipping program that you might want to look into as well.

25. Gold-N-Diamonds Inc.

This is a leading wholesaler and manufacturer of gold, silver, and diamond jewelry in the US.

26. Danforth Pewter

They are a manufacturer of pewter jewelry.

27. Wholesale Interiors

This is a wholesaler for interiors. In case in the future you think you're ready to venture into dropshipping larger products then you should check them out. They offer more than 1,500 different types of commercial and industrial furnishings.

28. Modloft

Modloft specializes in home furnishing. Their products include sofas, mattresses, bookcases, and beds among other things.

29. ISO Beauty

ISO Beauty is a manufacturer and distributor of beauty products such as shampoo, hair extensions, blow dryers, straighteners, and mineral makeup and a lot more. They have a good dropshipping program too.

30. Beauty Joint

Beauty Joint is a cosmetics wholesaler. They have an extensive collection of beauty products and Korean makeup.

Note that the list above is not an extensive one. There are literally hundreds of popular wholesalers, manufacturers, and directories. At least you have somewhere to start at this point in case you're looking for suppliers and manufacturers.

Contacting the Supplier, Wholesaler, or Manufacturer

At this point you should create a list of manufacturers and wholesalers that carry the products that you want to sell. Check out their contact information and you can send them an email or call them if they have their phone number listed.

Visit their official website and see if they have a contact form. If they do then fill it out and ask them to contact you. Leave your email and phone number in the form so they can get back to you.

Email

Sending an email will be a more convenient option. You don't have to sit and wait for someone to answer the phone.

And you don't get the runaround too. But if they do give you the runaround then it isn't a good wholesaler/supplier.

When do contact them ask for the following:

- Details about the particular products that you are interested in selling
- Any fees that you should compute with each order
- Customer service options
- Returns and cancellations
- ETDs and delivery details
- Warranties and return guarantees
- Any discounts that you can take advantage of or whatever they want to offer

What to Ask Over the Phone

Here is a list of questions that you should ask over the phone. Remember to sound like a true blue entrepreneur, when you talk to their reps. First impressions are important.

1. What payment terms are available? Can they be negotiated?
2. Do you sell direct? (if they say yes they sell directly to the general public then they're a scam—more on that later)
3. Are there any costs other than the cost of the product?
4. What is the expected gross margin?

5. What is your company's return policy?
6. What kind of money back guarantee or warranty that you offer?
7. When would the prices likely change?
8. Can your service reps answer product inquiries?
9. Do you manufacture custom items? (ask this if you're contacting an actual manufacturer and not just a wholesaler)
10. Does your company provide a data feed?

Steady your voice when you talk to a representative of a wholesaler or manufacturer. These people are interested in looking for business partners—so act like one. They will be more interested in key players and entrepreneurs who will work with them for the long haul.

Now, if you sound like you don't know what you're talking about (i.e. a newbie) then these guys can take advantage of the situation and charge you higher rates. It's either that or they won't talk or respond to you.

Avoid Fakes and Scams

Unfortunately, where there is money to be made, there will be unscrupulous people who will try to take advantage of unsuspecting people. Here are a few warning signs that you should pay attention to.

- ***Ask if they sell to the public***

A real wholesaler will not sell their goods to the public. They are not a B2C type of business—they're B2B! There is no sense why they would do that. If they slip and they tell you that they also sell directly to the public then they are probably a retailer.

They're one of those retailers that say they sell at "wholesale prices." Yeah right. A lot of times they actually have inflated prices.

- ***No BBB listing***

If the supplier or wholesaler is based in the US then it should be listed in the BBB. The BBB is where consumers report frauds. If they have a bad rap on BBB then you will most likely see them. If they have a good reputation on the BBB or if they tend to resolve issues and complaints quickly then you will that recorded there as well.

- ***They don't take credit cards***

Why wouldn't they? You will find some suppliers that only take direct bank transfers. If that is the case then look for someone else. Almost every real wholesaler will take credit card payments.

- ***Membership fees and monthly fees***

There are legit suppliers and wholesalers who do charge monthly fees. But not all of them do. If they do charge a fee, make the effort to ask why they charge this fee. If they give an honest sounding answer like data and other exclusive services that they offer to members then you can try it for one month.

If the added services are worth it then stay. You can even opt to pay for the entire thing for a whole year, which usually saves you a lot of money. If they give you some crazy reason or they don't have any reason for charging you a membership fee then walk away.

- ***No address displayed***

Not providing a business address is a big red flag for any dropshipper. How do you know where the products are coming from? If you want to estimate the ETD of your deliveries how do you do that if you don't have a clue where the warehouses are?

- ***Call the number listed on their website***

Worst case scenario that the supplier doesn't have a phone number posted. Why not? If the number doesn't work—then they either aren't updated on their phone bills or the phone number is fake.

If someone answers ask them the questions listed earlier. If it takes them a while to answer your questions or if their answers aren't satisfactory then take them off your list of potential suppliers.

- ***Contact the Manufacturer***

If you are able to get hold of a manufacturer then you can ask them about the wholesaler. Every manufacturer ought to know who their wholesalers are. They also have a list of their suppliers as well.

If the wholesaler is on the manufacturer's list then you know they're legit. If they aren't or the manufacturer doesn't know them then they're a scam.

Minimum Order Sizes

Some wholesalers will require minimum order sizes. Sometimes that will not make sense to a dropshipper. What if you only need to order 1 item but the minimum order size are 10?

Note that this minimum is for initial orders—a requirement for first timers. This is a tactic they use to protect themselves from so called window shopping merchants. These merchants tend to ask a lot of questions and only make very small orders but won't stay in business for long.

So what do you do if the minimum order is about $500 but your usual order size is only around $75 to $100? Don't pre-order the $500 worth of goods. You're a dropshipper not your run of the mill ecommerce retailer. You don't want to have items on hand as stock.

What you can do is to call the manufacturer or wholesaler and pay for a $500 pre-pay credit. This amount will then be applied to your first few orders.

That is a show of faith to the wholesaler or supplier that you are in it for the long haul—which is what they want in the first place. It also shows that you are serious in your commitment to their business.

Understanding Payment Options

The majority of suppliers and wholesalers use either 2 payment options:

1. Credit Cards
2. Net Terms

Credit Cards

When you're just starting out in dropshipping your main go to payment method would be to use a credit card. Remember that in a previous chapter we mentioned that you should get a business credit card for your dropshipping business.

Note that even after you have made a thriving enterprise out of dropshipping you will still need to use your business credit card as a payment option. In many cases it will be your best option.

As you can see, a credit card is a very convenient option. On top of that since you will be making a lot of purchases you will eventually be racking up a lot of rewards points.

Note that you won't be incurring these expenses out of your own pocket. First off this is your business credit card. Other than that the purchases that you will make have been paid off initially by your customers since they bought it off your site.

Net Terms

Net terms are payments that are usually made through bank draw or check. They're call net terms because they are term payments. For instance, a supplier or wholesaler gives you net 30 terms. That means you have 30 days after the date of purchase to send the payment for the item that was purchased.

In short you are given a line of credit for the items that you will purchase. You will be required to submit credit references if you want to setup net terms with a supplier. You will also be required to submit documentation and the wholesaler will look into your credit history and your credit score as well.

Chapter 9: Marketing Your Store

In the previous chapters we have covered the different sales channels that you can choose from. We have also gone over how to find suppliers that will provide you with products to sell. We have also gone over the details of branding your business.

In this chapter we will go over the huge brunt of the grunt work that lies ahead. Assuming that you have already done all the things that were described in the previous chapters, the next thing you need to do is to market your store.

You have your store and your own branding. Now the goal is to establish brand awareness and capture potential leads that you can convert into actual customers. Note that you can view this chapter as an extension of branding your business—but this time you're actually doing marketing.

Creating Buyer Personas

What's a buyer persona? A buyer persona is a detailed description of the ideal customers of your dropshipping store. Remember that you can't serve everyone. You need to segment your target market—you need to really zero in on who you want to sell to.

With buyer personas, you can understand which people you need to reach out to. This will eventually make marketing your business a lot easier. In short, buyer personas tell you who your customers are and what they want from your dropshipping store.

How Many Buyer Personas Do You Need?

The short and sweet answer to that question is it all depends on you. Just remember that the best buyer personas are created according to your market research. There is no magic number that I can actually give you.

However, a lot of businesses and small startup companies usually focus on 3 to 8 buyer personas. That should be enough to keep you busy. But if you are just starting out you should focus on 1 to 3.

For instance, you can't design your dropshipping store to attract elderly retirees, pro MMA fighters, top level executives, and stay at home moms at the same time. You need to focus on each of these market segments one at a time and build each corresponding section of your store according to their needs and wants.

It's up to you. But start with a few at first. Or you can just stick with one and work your way up from there.

How to Create Buyer Personas

Here are the steps so you can create your buyer personas.

1. Research Your Desired Audience

Go back to the products that you want to sell. Do some research about who actually buys them. Yes, this is all about niche marketing again. Are you interested in selling sporting goods? Which type of sporting goods? MMA equipment?

Now that you have narrowed things down define which age group actually buys this type of equipment. Where do they live? What is their income bracket (to help you with pricing).

We have gone over some tools in chapter 3 of this book that you can use such as Google Trends and Keyword Planner. They can help you see what keywords people are using to search for related products to your niche.

2. Narrow down the details

Use the same tools to narrow down the characteristics of your ideal customer. Consider the following:

- Email preferences (how often do they read their emails)
- Challenges they face
- Their interests
- Skill levels
- Interests
- What books are they reading
- Their age
- Their job

3. Create Personas and Give Them Names

Going back to our example, we are looking to sell to people who are interested in MMA equipment. We need to categorize each possible customer that we will have. We will then name each one of them.

For instance let's call one persona the Grappler, here are possible characteristics of the grappler persona:

- Age 18 to 40+
- Mid-range income
- Comes from different cultural backgrounds
- Doesn't mind buying slightly more expensive equipment—they prefer quality over price
- Usual equipment that they will need include grappling mats, gis, spats, shorts, long sleeve tops, mouth guards, knee supports, ankle supports, and weights and weight training equipment

4. Focus your marketing content according to the Different Buyer Personas

Your next step is to plan your marketing according to the buyer personas that you have crafted. You should also research all the related products and brands as well.

Raw Marketing—Low Cost Strategies

Now that you have buyer personas in mind, your dropshipping store, your selected products, and now it's time to post your product list. You will be basically building content on your dropshipping site.

As you grow your content you also need to infuse low cost marketing strategies. These will help promote your site and also your products without incurring huge overhead and other expenses.

Displayed Ads

Display ads are more than just the annoying banners on the side or the top of your site. Well, you're setting up an online store so people will expect some form of advertising. Here are a couple of tips when choosing which ads you would like to post on each page:

- **Be mindful where you put them**: don't splash ads everywhere on your site. It will annoy your site visitors to death. Look at how Amazon and other big name sites do it.

  They have lots of useful information first and then a few relevant product links and images (the actual ads) at the top, bottom, and somewhere in the middle as well.

  Don't put ads that pop up over and over again. People don't want to be constantly reminded that you are trying to sell to them.

- **Let the ads be about your customers**: it is a rule of thumb that no one likes to be sold to. If people notice that you are pushing your products too much then they will tend to leave.

The solution is to provide them with solutions and benefits. Remember that you have identified specific needs when you created your buyer personas. Use that info when crafting the short statements that you will show in your short video clips, images, and gifs to advertise your products.

Make it look like a product that you are advertising is there to solve a problem or pain that they may be having at the moment. In the case of a grappler, you can advertise a new grappling instructional DVD set about beating a larger and stronger opponent.

For pros and higher level grapplers, you can offer particular types of competition gis that are lighter and sturdier which helps them perform better during competition.

Address needs and answer questions in the ads that you display.

Standard SEO

Search engine optimization increases your dropshipping site's visibility. With good SEO practices, anyone interested in a product that your ecommerce site carries can find it with a simple Google search.

But sometimes that is easier said than done. There are a lot of elements involved in good SEO. Basically there are two types of SEO that you need to accomplish—on page SEO and off page SEO.

On Page SEO

On page SEO are the things that you can do on your dropshipping site that can help put it in the first 3 pages of search results when people look for stuff on Google or other search engines.

Things might get slightly technical in the next section—only slightly. Here are the website elements that you need to work on:

- **Title Tags** – these are tags that you put on certain texts of each web page on your site. They tell search engines that this is the title of this particular page. A title tag should focus on the keyword that people use to search for the product that you are selling. If you're selling grappling mats, then your related page titles should have that title tag and the keyword you want to use inside it.

- **Meta Description** – this is what comes up as a short description of the item that you searched for on Google. Here's an example of that:

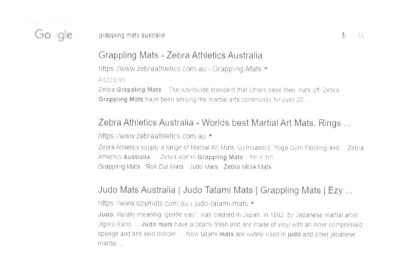

The text in blue is the link to the specific web page or site. The green line that starts with "https:" or "http" is the actual link or URL of the said site. The short text after that is the meta description. It tells your readers what that page is all about.

They base their decisions whether to click on your link or not depending on the short snippet that you put in there. If you make that snippet of text convincing enough then you can invite (or entice) them to open that page.

- **Headings** – search engines love headings and subheading even on online retailing sites. They improve the readability of your page which benefits customers and it benefits your page ranking as well.

- **Keywords** – we have talked about keywords and keyword research in a separate chapter. Just remember that you should use the keywords that you researched on your product pages, blog posts, and other informational pages on your site.

- **Content** – the very content that you post on each product should be helpful to the customer. You should include product details, reviews, specs, and other information that will help shoppers decides whether they will want to buy that product or not.

On Page SEO Tools

The good news is that there tools that you can use to evaluate your site's content and make on page SEO easier. That way you don't forget a single detail. These tools can help you find trending keywords, analyze your keyword use, find out how many times your chosen keywords have been used in a specific period of time, and a lot of other useful features.

Here are some of the tools that you might want to read about:

- Yoast SEO

- Rank Math
- SEOPress
- All in One SEO Pack
- SEOPressor
- The SEO Framework
- Premium SEO Pack
- WP Meta SEO
- Ahrefs SEO Keyword Tool
- Google Search Console
- SEMRush
- KWFinder
- Moz SEO Software
- Ubersuggest
- Answer The Public (this one's free)
- SpyFu
- Woorank
- Majestic
- Google Trends
- SEOQuake (this one is free too)
- Siteliner
- Fat Rank
- Keywords Everywhere
- Screaming Frog
- CORA

Off Page SEO

Off page SEO refers to the things that affect your search ranking that are not directly in your control. This is what everyone else on the internet does to link to or talk about your dropshipping website.

Now, off page SEO is a huge topic in itself that will warrant a lot of your time and effort. Again, you can hire a freelancer to do your off page SEO for you at first but you will have to learn how to do it yourself along the way.

Here are some of the off-page SEO strategies that you can employ:

- **Link building** – other sites linking to your site and your pages.

- **Social media marketing** (we'll cover this later)

- **Guest blogging** – this is when you contact other website owners and bloggers so that you can talk about a subject that you know very well (like the products that you are marketing) and then you can link and advertise your site or social media channels on that blog post. This requires some negotiation and sometimes you have to pay so you can have guest posts on other people's sites.

- **Brand mentions in other sites and social media portals**

- **Influencer marketing** – this is another huge topic in itself. This is the cyber equivalent of a celebrity endorsement of your site or product. Sometime in the future you can contact authorities and influencers that have huge followings (like maybe a celebrity, a popular athlete, an actual expert on a given subject etc.).

  You will then work with them to promote a cause or talk about a subject matter. You can then do some namedropping and mention your store somewhere in there. The influencer (the one that you working with) has fans and followers on social media and elsewhere. They can be influenced to go see your dropshipping store and see what you have to offer. Again there are more details about influencer marketing than what we can squeeze into this book.

Note that off page SEO is a long term strategy. It is not something that you can do in just a month or a few days. You need to establish your dropshipping site's reputation so that people will trust and talk about it.

Shotgun/Machine Gun Method for SMM

This is what I call the less effective and laborious method of doing social media marketing (SMM). What is the shotgun or machine gun method?

Well here it is. This is where you talk to your friends and family on social media and post links to your dropshipping site. You ask them to visit it and give it a try.

You also create a Facebook page, Instagram account, YouTube channel, and other social media accounts and you promote your ecommerce site there. You add people, follow people, talk to people online, and post links everywhere in the hopes that you will gain visitors to your site.

This is low cost because you aren't spending anything. However, it is laborious as you can see. It can also annoy the heck out of people since you keep posting about your business.

You target anyone and everyone on social media ergo shotgun or machine gun. Does it work? Yes it might on occasion. The problem is that it isn't a targeted method. But at least it is free.

Mid-to High Cost Marketing

The next marketing strategies that we will cover will cost you some money. Some are more costly than others. I suggest that you should turn to these options after you have done everything that you can through on-page SEO. A lot of the strategies that we will cover will include pay per click platforms, which include the following:

- Facebook Ads

- Google AdWords
- Instagram Ads
- Twitter Ads
- Pinterest Ads

Facebook Ads

Why use Facebook Ads? Facebook can be a tricky social media platform to navigate if you're trying to market your products there. But it is not something that you should dismiss outright.

Their 2 billion worldwide subscribers across different demographics is no small thing. On top of that they also own Instagram (another important portal that you should market too as well) and Messenger.

What you have here is a lot of engaged and also active traffic from actual users. With the analytics tools that Facebook can provide you can target different customers based on behaviors, interests, and other demographics.

Facebook is also a great place to get a foothold of your brand awareness. You can customize your own Facebook page, link it to your dropshipping store, create Facebook groups that will provide chatter for your products (and promote them there too), and create a following for your company.

There are online marketers who have given up on Facebook because of the confusing number of ad options that they offer. Sometimes they get so confused or frustrated that they never really get to setup an actual ad campaign.

So here's how you get things right from the start.

1. Setup Your Facebook Business Manager Account

The first step is to setup your Business Manager account on Facebook. All you need to do is to go to this link: https://business.facebook.com/

And then, after that you need to click the blue Create Account button on the top right.

You will be required to enter a few important details like your business name (you should have setup your business, remember?), your email address, and of course your name.

Follow the prompts that you will see on the screen. You will get a walk through such as adding an advertising account (if you don't have one yet), i.e. an Ad Account. And then you will connect that business account to your Facebook business page.

2. Install Facebook Pixel

We will discuss Facebook Pixel in a later section of this chapter. For now just remember that Facebook Pixel is a tool (it's actually lines of code that you need to add to your ecommerce website) that you can use to track you customers' activities on your dropshipping platform.

You can set it up on Shopify and other third party retailers as well. Unfortunately, this isn't exactly possible in Amazon and eBay.

3. Create a Facebook Ad Campaign

The next step is to create an Ad campaign. These campaigns will include carousels, videos, and images. These will be shown on Facebook as something that is "sponsored."

Here are the steps to create one:

> Create an objective. Open your Business Manager account and then go to Ad Manager. Click on the Create button. Select an objective. You will see a table that shows three different categories for your new

objective, which includes: Awareness, Consideration, and Conversion.

Each of these categories has a few options under there. Choose the appropriate objective that you want to achieve for this ad campaign.

Next you need to set your ad sets. You will be asked to identify your target audience, your budget for your ad campaign, and the ad placement. Follow the prompts as you go.

You may be prompted to add more details for the ad that you are making. For example, you chose Conversion as the objective. You will be asked regarding conversion details.

Note that the conversion events that Facebook can use will depend on the events that their system can scan on your website. If you haven't had any add to carts or actual purchases made on your site then Facebook Ads can't optimize for such events or they may not be available yet for your ad campaign.

To work around this, you should switch objectives and choose Traffic instead. This will help to optimize future purchase events that may happen.

4. Set Your Budget

When you're asked about the budget for that ad, you will need to enter the cost of the product, the amount of the budget you are willing to spend, the type of objective (sales objectives will cost more compared to brand awareness campaigns), and the average cost you estimate for each time you acquire a customer.

Audience Section

Go to the audience section to specify the audience that you want the ads to target.   You will need to specify location, language spoken, age, gender, interests, behaviors, demographics, and other specific details.

Connection Type

Select a connection type. Your options include people who like your page, friends, people who have used your app and others.

Placements

You will then have to specify where you want your ads to be placed. This will specify which newsfeeds your ads will appear. This is where you can also specify if you want to target Instagram users as well.

Selecting Your Ad

Next you need to select the ad itself. This is called a Facebook Creative. Here are the ads that you can choose from:

1. Single Image Ad – this is image ads that we see on websites and pretty much everywhere. Marketers used to focus on static images for a long time but now they have switched to video.

But single image ads still have a powerful impact especially when they are placed in the right places.

They should have the following key elements:

- A call to action (e.g. learn more, subscribe now, shop now etc.)
- Newsfeed link on the description that will expand when clicked (you can add this or not, it's up to you)
- Destination URL (i.e. a landing page or a social media link)
- Text should appear at the top of the pic
- Image aspect ratio should be anywhere from 1:1 to 16:9

Combine images with compelling copy to build curiosity about your products/brand. Let your images be teasers. Remember the following with your images:

- Third party testimonials

- Reviews from actual customers
- Extra page links
- Use entertaining and relevant emojis with the description
- Choose a relatable subject matter
- Select images that encourages engagement

2. Single Video Ad – this includes videos, Facebook Watch, IGTV, and others. Video is already the number one ad format today. Good video ads have the following key elements:

- Call to action
- Newsfeed link
- Destination URL
- Display URL (this is a link/URL that will appear above the video headline—usually your dropshipping store's domain)
- Text that appear above the video
- The video can either have a horizontal or vertical orientation
- Recommended aspect ratio is either 1:1 or 16:9

3. *Carousel Ad* – a carousel is a series of images or videos (or a combination of both) that you scroll left to right.

Successful carousel ads have the following key elements:

- Call to action
- Newsfeed link (optional)
- Headline below the image/video in bold text
- Display URL
- Descriptive text above the video/image carousel
- Recommended aspect ratio is 1:1
- 10 square videos/images maximum in the carousel (anything longer and you will lose your audience)

4. Collection Ad – A collection ad is also a combination of video and images. But it is formatted differently. It usually comes with a long form video and a collection of images underneath it. The images usually are catalog images of your product (the same images you use on your dropshipping site).

This is a powerful ad format. You have video that captures the consumer's attention and the catalog helps to increase interest in your product.

Here are the key elements for collection ads:

- A custom Instant Experience (explained later)
- Collection images
- Video or a main image (known as the hero image)
- Recommended aspect ratio is 1:1 or 16:9
- Descriptive text (copywriting) above the image

5. Instant Experience – this is not really a new type of ad. It's actually an ad element. You can add an instant experience to a video, image, carousel, and others. It's a pop up page that comes up when a user taps or clicks on the call to action that you added.

Think of it as a landing page inside Facebook or Instagram. You can use instant experiences to test which of your ads get more attention from leads and customers—some sort of an A/B test.

Launch two of these (use different formats) and see which one gets more views. The one that gets more views should be replicated in the future.

Instagram Marketing

Since Instagram is owned by Facebook, a lot of the tools that you use in Facebook marketing will also be available on Instagram. You can also use the same ad formats/types (i.e. Creatives) here as well.

How Many Followers Do You Really Need?

You can call this the golden question on Instagram. The quick and easy answer is that it's not as many as you think. You certainly don't need thousands upon thousands of Instagram followers to make money on dropshipping using Instagram ads.

But there's a long answer—it depends (drum roll). There are several factors that you need to consider, which includes the following:

- How high is your engagement
- Revenue channels you are exploring
- Your niche

Linking Issues

One of the problems that you will encounter in Instagram is the limited capability to link to your dropshipping site or directly to your product pages. What you need to do is to invite users to view your bio and your link will be on that bio. You can't put links on your posts. You can't use your photos or videos as links.

However, for many companies this has been a huge source of Instagram traffic and a lot of dropshippers have seen a lot of success from that. **Rule of Thumb** – don't forget to put the URL of your dropshipping site or product page on your Instagram bio.

Now, there is another place where you can put a link to your ecommerce store on Instagram. If you advertise on Instagram then you are allowed to put a link on the Shop Now button of your post/ad. And that is another source of traffic for you.

Partnering with Shopify

Instagram has now entered a deal with Shopify. Now customers can directly shop on Instagram by clicking on a product you advertised and that will instantly lead them to your Shopify store and go to checkout.

It's called the Instagram Feed and Slider Pro, which you can find by going to: https://apps.shopify.com/instagram-feed-pro?surface_detail=trending-apps&surface_inter_position=2&surface_intra_position=4&surface_type=home

It comes with a 7 day free trial so you can test the add-on/app without any obligations to sign up. Its regular rate is $3.99 a month.

Advertising on Instagram

The old way of advertising on Instagram was to negotiate with influencers (Instagram accounts with a huge following) so that they will promote your product on their feed. It's usually an expensive method and there is very little targeting done. This still works though so you might want to consider it in the future.

Things have changed since 2015 and now Facebook's advertising platform has literally taken over Instagram (they own it, remember?). Some of the advantages of these changes include:

- Refined audience targeting
- Report tracking
- The use of Instants (discussed earlier)
- Scalable pricing (wider pricing options)

Types of Instagram Ads

Again, the ads on Instagram are pretty much the same ones you use on Facebook. They include photo ads, video ads, and carousel ads. On top of those three, there are a couple of unique ads on this social media platform that you need to pay attention as well: slideshow ads and stories ads.

Slideshow Ads

These ads are made up of a series of still images (ergo a slideshow) and they play like a video.

Stories Ads

Instagram stories are similar to Facebook stories. They're posts that only appear for a time instead of getting posted on your timeline. They're also similar to the stories that you can find on Snapchat. According to a lot of case studies people tend to remember these stories (even the ads they have seen there) a lot longer.

Instagram Ad Objectives

You remember the Objectives on Facebook? They have them here too. However, they are a little different on Instagram. The options are:

- Conversions
- Lead generation
- Video views
- Engagement
- App installs
- Traffic
- Reach
- Brand awareness

App installs of course are for increasing your dropshipping app installs—yes, you can develop your own app for mobile devices. Lead generation is purely for collecting user or viewer information.

How to Create Instagram Ads

1. Link your Instagram account to your Facebook account
2. Create an Instagram Ad campaign
3. Create your ad set
4. Analyze and optimize your ads

You have already seen steps 1 to 3 when we went over how to advertise on Facebook. It's pretty much the same process. Open your Facebook business page and then go to Instagram Ads. Click login and then enter your Instagram logins.

After that you open Ad Manager and that is where you can create your ad campaigns. You will then create your ad sets – i.e. your Creatives along with your selected audience. Finally you set your budget.

Analyze and Optimize

After you launch your first ad, which is the hardest part. You need to watch the analytics. See how many clicks you're getting. You can then create a second ad and compare which one is better.

You can create an image ad first. Then try a carousel or collection. Give each one a week or two for testing. While waiting for the results you can then craft a short video ad. Test each one to see which ones work better for your products.

Twitter Marketing

You will basically go through the same process for Twitter marketing. We've covered a lot of the same in the previous chapters. You need to create buyer personas (i.e. your target audience), create content that is engaging and unique (i.e. your brands and info posts), schedule and organize your posts, and then finally analyze and impact the results.

Twitter can be your go to place for customer service and also for product announcements. It is free to use and you can use it for your branding efforts. You can also use it to find prospects and also look into what your competitors are doing.

Brand Your Profile

Follow your branding strategy/plan when you customize your Twitter account. Use your log and images on your profile. Use taglines that promote your business and your products. Here are the parts of your Twitter profile that you need to customize:

- Handle (your @username)
- Header (background image)
- Profile picture (usually your store's logo)
- Bio (tell something about your business)
- URL (usually your store's URL)
- Birthday (when did you start your dropshipping business)

Create Lists

You can organize your followers into lists. You can create lists for premium customers, your employees, your business partners, etc. This helps you follow specific accounts especially influencers that you can convince to promote your business.

Host Twitter Chats

Announce two weeks ahead or more that you are hosting a Twitter chat. It's an event where you can promote a product or discuss a subject that is related to your niche. This creates a sense of community among your followers. You can even talk about things that you are working on.

To host a chat event, set a time, hashtag, date, and topic. You can Tweet that and also post it on your website. Ask your followers to use your hashtag too.

Twitter Ads

Now, this is where free stuff on Twitter ends. But note that you can get a lot of things going for your dropshipping business by just constantly Tweeting and following other businesses, organizations, and people who have a stake in your niche.

Create an Ad Account

The first step of course is to create an Ad Account. You can do that by going here:

https://ads.twitter.com/login

After creating an account you can login and you will see the options on your dashboard. Your next step is to create an ad campaign by clicking the Create New Campaign button.

Types of Twitter Ads

There are several types of Twitter ads that you can choose from:

- **Followers** – select this if you're just starting out. This ad type increases your number of followers and improves brand awareness.
- **Webclicks/Conversions** – this is the type of ad for increasing traffic to your site. This one will allow you to use conversion tracking tag so you can check data about people who visit your site on Twitter. You can choose to track different activities like purchases, site visits, sign ups, and downloads, etc.
- **App Installs** – this is the ad type if you want to track data about people who install your app.
- **Leads** – this ad type allows you to capture email addresses and other information about potential leads. You can offer email subscriptions, coupon

codes, eBooks, buyer's guides, info materials, and others in exchange for their information.

- **Promoted Tweets** – these are the types of tweets that come with paid promotions. These are the tweets that end up at the top of search results, on promoted pages, your profile page (or the timelines of your target market), official Twitter clients, and they are shown to people who haven't followed your account yet.

Note that there is a trends widget that you can use in Twitter but it is way too expensive so I didn't include it here. Unless you have a budget of $200,000 (or higher) then you might want to stay away from this tool for now.

Targeting Your Audience

You can specify how your ads target your desired audience. Remember to follow the demographic characteristics that you have set in your buyer personas. Here are your options when you create your ads:

Location – you can select the specific location of the audience that you want to target. You can also choose to show your ads to all targeted locations.

Gender – select the gender of your target audience

Language – select the targeted language

Device and Platforms – you can select the type of devices where your ads can be displayed. This will depend on the type of operating system used in the said devices.

Keyword Targeting – you can indicate keywords that people use on Twitter. Your ads will then be displayed in searches made by users who use the same keywords. Use the keywords that you have determined using your Keyword Planner and Google Trends.

Targeting by Followers – there is a reason why you need to research your competitors. Find them on Twitter and then put them in this targeted list. What happens here is that Twitter will post your ads on their followers' timelines. You can also list topics that you shared and that competitors are also tweeting about. Twitter will then find companies that tweet on the same topics and your ads can then be displayed on their timelines as well.

Target by Interest – this is where your niche selection comes in. There are interest categories that you can use to determine your target audience. Some of these targeted interests include food and drink, gaming, family and parenting, careers, business, books and literature, etc. Your ads will then be shown to users who have these interests.

Set Your Budget

As usual, you should select a budget for your ad campaigns. This is the section where you enter your payment details.

The good news here is that there is no minimum spend and you only pay for actual replies, clicks, retweets, follows, and other engagement activities with your ads. Note that you can start and stop an ad campaign any time. Once you have set this up your ad campaigns will start to run – which means they will be displayed to your targeted audience.

Analyze Performance

Once your ad campaigns are up and running, you will see their performance charts on the main campaign screen. Here you can review performance of each ad according to the options that you selected such as location, language, demographics, interest, etc.

Here is what that screen looks like:

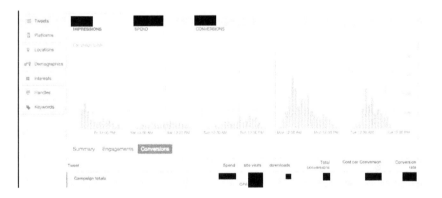

Okay so I kind of removed some of the data there. As you can see from that screen you can see how each of your campaigns have performed in different time periods, which ones performed well, and how much you spent for each campaign.

You can then adjust the advertising methods accordingly.

Pinterest Marketing

Of course Facebook and Instagram get a lot of attention nowadays. But you can't count out Pinterest as a marketing avenue for your dropshipping business. Remember that your potential and current customers are visual creatures. That is why Pinterest and Instagram are powerful marketing tools.

Just like Twitter, Pinterest may not have as large a following like Facebook and Instagram. But their users number in the millions—a huge market nonetheless. There are 250 million people who browse Pinterest each month (they're called "pinners").

Again, the initial strategy is the same. Determine your buyer personas, create relevant and engaging content based on those personas, post regularly, optimize your posts for search engine optimization, use hashtags, and use other similar strategies.

Multiple Pins - Multiple Spins - Same Post

On Pinterest you're using "pins" – which are essentially photos and videos. You can actually use multiple pins or a collection of pins in one post. You usually want to use photos and videos that have a common theme.

Use Seasonal Trends

This is a technique that you can take advantage of later when you have established a following. But you can also use it to jump start your ecommerce store. You can launch your store weeks before the holidays and promote your products ahead of time.

This is particularly effective in Pinterest where people tend to gravitate to pins during holidays and other special occasions. Best practice dictates that you should time your pins 30 to 45 days in advance.

Pay Attention to the Top 100 Trends

Pinterest also releases its list of top 100 trends each year. You should check out their list and see if your niche fits into any of the trends for a given year. If it is then that is a clear indicator that there might be a lot of interest in your products.

Use Rich Pins

Rich Pins are pins on Pinterest that include extra information in them. They are free to use and they can help provide more information about what your store offers. It's great for spreading brand awareness and customer education.

There are 4 types of Rich Pins that you can use:

- Article Rich Pins – they include a story description, author name, and a headline
- App Pins – this Rich Pin is only available on devices running iOS. These pins include an "install now" button so users can directly install an app on their iOS devices.
- Recipe Pins – this Rich Pin can include serving sizes, cooking times, and recipes.
- Product Pins – this Rich Pin highlights the availability of a product, its real time price, and where to buy them.

For a dropshipping store, your initial Rich Pin should be a Product Pin. But if you have an app, and informational articles then you can use those for brand awareness as well. If your niche has something to do with cooking, baking etc. then the Recipe Pins may be useful to you.

Create a Business Account

Before you can use Rich Pins you need to create a Pinterest Business account. If you already have an account you can upgrade it to a business account. However, I would suggest that you just create a new business account rather than mix your business and personal accounts.

To convert an existing account in Pinterest, you need to follow the steps provided here:

https://www.pinterest.com/business/convert/

If you're creating a new business account then go here:

https://www.pinterest.com/business/create/

Once your account has been created, you will be given access to your very own business profile. Note that just like in other social media channels, Pinterest also has its own analytics tools.

Add Your Details

The next step is to add the details to your profile. That means your handle, your profile picture (usually with your company logo on it), location, and other useful information.

Claiming Your Website

Claiming your website allows you to attribute any pin created from your site whether you created it yourself or an employee does it for you. Claiming is done by adding a meta tag on your website. There is an HTML file that you need to add to the index of your site.

Now, if you don't know how to do that then here are instructions from Pinterest on how you can do that along with different downloadable HTML files that you can use for different web hosts:

https://help.pinterest.com/en/business/article/claim-your-website

Pinterest Widgets

The next step is to add Pinterest widgets on your site. It allows you to add a Save button on your site so that people can easily pin your page or product on Pinterest. It also allows you to add follow buttons, and embed pins to make pinning your content on social media a lot easier.

The good news is that Pinterest has created its very own widget builder that you can use. You can find details about it by going here:

https://business.pinterest.com/en/pinterest-widget-builder

Analytics Tools

Just like Facebook Pixel (more on that later), Pinterest also has its own performance tracking tool that you can install on your site. It's called Pinterest Tag. You can find details about it and how to install it on your site by going here:

https://business.pinterest.com/en/pinterest-tag

This tool allows you to do the following:

- Build new audiences
- Measure the performance of your ad campaigns
- Keep track of conversions (see which type of pinner clicks your promoted pins and what they do on your site—which allow you to figure out who actually buys your products).

You can find that and the other analytics tools on Pinterest by going to this page:

https://analytics.pinterest.com/

Facebook Pixel—Retargeting Like a Sniper

Your ecommerce site should have Facebook Pixel on it. What is Pixel? It is Facebook's retargeting advertising system—just a fancy way to say you're following up on current and potential leads. As it was explained earlier, this is a lot like **Pinterest Tag** (described earlier) that allows you to determine exactly who your actual audience or market really is.

Well, you see, getting likes, shares, and follows on Facebook is great and all but they aren't a guarantee that such activity will translate to sales. What you need to do is to have the ability to pinpoint the people who don't just interact with your posts but those who actually check out your products and place items on their shopping carts.

And that is where Facebook Pixel comes into play. Taking out all the technical jargon, Pixel is a bunch of code that you can add to your dropshipping site. It monitors people that go to your site, track what they do there, and also find out what they do on Facebook that relates to your business.

On top of that, the algorithm for Pixel creates what is called the Facebook LAA. Yes, the jargons just keep coming. LAA is short for Look Alike Audiences. What this means is that Facebook will make use of their humongous data about their users.

Pixel will create a profile of the people who actually bought something from you or at least fiddled around with their shopping carts even if they didn't actually buy something.

Let's say there were 30 people who visited your site through Facebook or some other link. Pixel will try to make a profile of the people who interacted with your site based on their activities both on Facebook and on your site as well.

Facebook will then find people with the same activities and interests using their site's data. They will become your targeted potential audience. Your ads will then be shown to people on Facebook that fit this profile.

The basis for this potential customer profile will be the people who purchased something on your site, those initiated the checkout process, or at least those who added products to their cart.

That's basically the gist of how Facebook Pixel works. It's definitely better at zeroing in on actual people who may actually buy something from your site.

It is definitely better than using a shotgun method. What I mean by that is just posting your content on Facebook everywhere. Prospecting to everyone and hoping that they will visit your site and buy something.

What is Facebook Pixel

Okay let's get a bit more technical—just a little. We're not going to go over the Javascript code or any coding that was done create Pixel and to explain how it does what it is doing.

Pixel is actually an analytics tool that was created by Facebook (obviously). Its primary purpose is to measure the effectiveness of your marketing efforts.

The very first use that you can take advantage of is to help you understand exactly what actions people are doing when they visit your ecommerce website. The end goal as stated earlier is to find and reach out to your target audiences.

Given all of that, if you are planning on using Facebook Ads or if you have already used them (and maybe you're not getting much success from them) then you should try out Facebook Pixel.

It's an affordable solution and it can potentially get you the most out of your social advertising budget.

What Does It Actually Do

Again, we now know that Pixel is just code that you add to your website. Think of it as a widget or an app that you can use for marketing and customer analytics. It actually does the following things:

- First it will track any conversions that have occurred using Facebook ads.
- It will then optimize the ads that you want to place based on the data it has collected or tracked.
- This tool will then look for and build targeted audiences for your future ad campaigns.
- The new ad campaigns will then target the actual people who interacted with your site—those who looked at products, placed them in the cart, and especially those who actually bought something.
- This tool uses cookies that track users both on Facebook and also on your ecommerce site.

Fine Tuning Your Facebook Ads Efforts

One of the best things that you will get out of Pixel is that it can help you fine tune your Facebook ads and become better at finding your targeted audience.

There will no longer be a need to reach out to anyone and everyone, which is laborious, tiring, and wasteful actually. The success rate of that social media marketing method is also quite low too.

With the help of the tracking data provided by Facebook, your ads on this social networking site will be seen by people who are more likely to buy from you. Their peers (the previous visitors of your site who bought goods) have the same needs as they do, which increases their chances of doing the same—which is the essence of Look Alike Audiences.

In short, Pixel will help to improve your ad conversion on Facebook. The end result is that you will get an increase in your return on investment.

Now, even if you are not yet using Facebook ads you should at least install Facebook Pixel on your site. At least you have something that will start tracking and gathering data about your site's visitors.

If you so choose to use Facebook ads later, then Pixel will already customer profiles and data ready for you to use. Pre-installing this tool is easy and your site usually won't experience any problems after installation.

Here are several ways how Facebook Pixel can help you improve your ad campaigns:

1. It Helps You Define Your Buying Audience

So you have several products on your ecommerce sites. You may even be running several dropshipping sites a few months from now. How do you know the age group that frequents a particular ecommerce site?

In other words you need to know the demographic of your actual buying audience. You also need to know where on planet earth they live. Is your market Asian? Are they North American? Are they European? Remember that each geo market group has different tastes and preferences. You need to appeal to those preferences to connect with your audience.

Other than figuring out all that pertinent info, Facebook Pixel can also help you identify what types of jobs they have. It can help you figure out pain points or challenges that they may be experiencing or trying to resolve.

Information such as Facebook usage, language, location, relationship status, education, gender, and age play key roles when gathering customer insights. These are important parts of analytics other than their purchasing activity. They will help you fine tune your ad and marketing efforts.

2. Marketing Goals

Okay so you have already identified your potential market on Facebook. Now, these aren't just your vanity market—you know the ones that just like and share your posts.

Remember that Pixel focuses on people who will actually buy your products. Pixel can help patch the holes in your marketing goals and campaigns.

Now every company or retailer will have different goals for each campaign that they will launch. Some are geared at improving brand awareness. Other campaigns will be designed for customer retention and increasing their loyalty. And yet other goals are set to increase lead generation—i.e. find more potential customers.

The biggest goal of course is to improve your bottom line—get more returns (aka to make more money).

You should make sure that every comment and every post that you make on your official Facebook page should support your current goals. Every ad should also support all the other activities that you do on this social media platform.

3. Helps You Formulate a Better Content Mix

You will fine tune your goals from time to time depending on the current needs of your business. One of the things that you need to plan is the right combination of content that you will publish on Facebook.

There are 2 fundamental content mix strategies that you can use when formulating your social media marketing plan. However, do take note that the data collected from the metrics produced by Pixel can help you decide what sort of content to use.

What are these 2 content mix strategies? They are the following:

- The Rule of Thirds
- The 80:20 Rule

Rule of Thirds: the rule of thirds talks about certain ratio between promotional posts and content that has value. This strategy is all about thirds—obviously. Simply put a third of your total posts should be ones that promote your business, the other third should be about personal interactions with your Facebook followers, and the final third of your total content should be shareable ideas and stories that may not be directly related to your business (but it should hold some relevance to your industry or niche).

The 80:20 Rule: this rule tells us that 80% of your Facebook posts should be entertaining, educational, and informative. The remaining 20% of your content mix should be the ones that actually promote your dropshipping store.

The idea behind this rule is to provide enough value to your audience so that they will be open to learning more about your business and of course your products. The goal here is to build relationships first and then to sell products after.

4. Redesign Your Facebook Page

Pixel can also help you fine tune your official Facebook page. You now know exactly the demographics of your buying followers. If there is anything on your Facebook page content that doesn't help to establish a relationship with that target market then you should take it down.

Note that you don't really need to make a page that will attract a million followers, like Coca Cola's. Though having that many followers will be a huge boost.

Facebook followers aren't the only factor that will indicate that your dropshipping business will be a success.

Conversion Tracking

This is one of the things that you should pay attention when using the analytics data provided by Facebook Pixel. It basically tells you how people actually interact with your dropshipping portal after seeing your Facebook ads.

It even allows you to track customers using different devices. It is a fact that there are some people who are more comfortable making purchases on mobile devices and there are those who still prefer to buy stuff using their computers.

There are those who will see your ads on their mobile devices and then switch to a desktop or laptop to make the actual purchase. And sometimes it is the other way around.

This information can help you fine tune your ad strategy. Let's say that the data reveals that your ads tend to attract more people who buy using their mobile phones. That means you should customize your ads for mobile devices— which means the design should be more streamlined for smaller screens.

So How Do I Use Facebook Pixel?

Remember that Facebook Pixel is all about tracking conversion events. What happens is that when someone sees your Facebook ad and clicks on it. It then leads them to your dropshipping website.

Pixel then tracks what that customer does on your site. If that site visitor buys something or at least puts items into his or her shopping cart then that person's data will be added to Pixel's analytic data.

That is an example of a conversion event. But that is not the only event that will be considered and collected by this tool. In fact, Facebook has a total of 17 predefined standard events.

An "event" in the eyes of Pixel is any of the 17 actions (this might change in the future so don't get hung up on the total number of these events—just call them events) that Facebook's analytics programmers have predefined.

Any action that a visitor does on your site after clicking your Facebook ad is called an event. Again, an example of an event is when a customer or visitor makes a purchase.

Standard Events

Okay so you want to know the standard events in Facebook Pixel? Here they are:

1. **Subscribe** – this is when a site visitor subscribes to your service or pays for your product.
2. **Submitting an Application** – this event occurs when a site visitor applies for something on your site. For instance, if you have a promotional program where customers need to apply for by submitting their emails for registration. That and other events like it are classified as an application that is submitted.
3. **Starting a Trial** – when a client or visitor starts a trial account or buys a trial/free/promotional product.
4. **Schedule** – when a visitor books an appointment (for service businesses)
5. **Find Location** – when a site visitor looks for your actual business address.

6. **Donate** – when a site visitor makes a donation for a cause that you are sponsoring.

7. **Customize Product** – this is triggered when a customer tweaks an order specifying or customizing a product or order such as the size, color, number of items, etc.

8. **Contact** – someone looks up your contact information or uses your contact form.

9. **View Content** – when someone lands or any page on your website.

10. **Search** – when a visitor uses the search function in your website.

11. **Initiate Checkout** – occurs when someone initiates the checkout process (it may or it may not turn out to be a completed sale).

12. **Add to Wish List** – occurs when someone adds a product to his/her wish list.

13. **Add to Cart** – occurs when a customer adds a product to their shopping cart (doesn't have to be a completed sale).

14. **Add Payment Information** – occurs when a person enters their payment information to buy something in your site.

15. **Complete Registration** – occurs when someone completes a subscription form or a registration form on your site.

16. **Lead** – occurs when someone identifies themselves as a potential lead by signing up for something like a free trial etc.

17. **Purchase** – occurs when a customer completes a purchase on your site.

Note that you can customize these standard events. Well, it's more like adding details to them rather than actually changing the basic settings. You can change details like the following:

- Basket contents
- ID
- Content type
- Currency
- The worth of a conversion event

You can use these tweaks to make Pixel track views of particular products on your website instead of just tracking any view/visit that is made. For example, if you sell pet supplies on your dropshipping site, you may want to check if you have more cat owners or dog owners visiting your site.

Custom Events

Now apart from the 17 standard events in Pixel back there, you are allowed to create an additional 100 other events that you customize. These will also be tracked by Pixel just like the standard 17.

This allows you to collect more details about the visitors of your site. You can create either events or track specific URLs on your site.

Keep in mind that the limit is 100 custom events/URLs. If you reach that many items and you want to add more you can just delete the old ones that you no longer use/need and add new ones.

You can use these rules so you can measure more specific actions by your site visitors. For instance, you can adjust settings to that Pixel will monitor purchases for a specific type of product (let's say dog collars) that are priced $15 and higher.

That means the system will collect data and find similar Facebook users who tend to do the same product preferences or buying behavior.

Here are the things that you can do with custom events:

- Control the custom conversion data only and not the entire data. You can actually share the data to your partners. This way you can limit and control the data that you share.
- It allows you to filter events—for instance you can track how many customers buy a particular shoe size or certain color of a product etc.
- It allows you to setup conversion events without having to write any programming code that will be added to your website.

- It optimizes ad delivery to specific types of leads using conversion data that has been gathered thus far.
- Optimize ad delivery.

Creating Facebook Pixel

Now that you know the advantages of Facebook Pixel and you might already have an idea about what type of data you want to track then it's time to learn how to create Pixel on your dropshipping site.

Here are the steps:

1. Create Pixel

Remember that pixel is nothing more than just code that you add to the header of your website. Open the Facebook Events Manager, which you can find here:

https://www.facebook.com/events_manager

Note that you should be logged into your Facebook account to open that page. Next you will need to go to the Pixels tab/section in Events Manager. Click the blue Get Started button.

A popup will appear which will give you options to create your pixel. There will also be a box where you can enter your site's URL. This will submit your site's URL for analysis to figure out what options are available for you.

You will also be a box called Pixel Name. It's just the custom name for your Facebook Pixel code. After entering that info click on Create Pixel. After that you should follow the rest of the prompts that will pop up along the way. It's pretty much automatic so you won't really have to worry about the actual code that will be generated.

2. Add Facebook Pixel to Your Website

After your own custom Facebook Pixel has been created the next step is to add it to your website. You several options on how to add Pixel to your website, which include the following:

a. If you have a web admin who updates your website for you, go to Setup Pixel. And then go to Email Instructions to a Developer. You will then be prompted to enter your web admin's/developer's email address. And then finally click Save.

b. Now, if you are the one who manages your website—meaning you are the web admin or site developer—Go to Pixels > Manually Install Pixel Code Yourself. After that, open your website's header. Find the header tag of your website and then copy the entire code that you see on the Events Manager page. Remember that this code should be inserted just before the closing header tag (i.e. </head>). Finally, update your site.

After the code has been saved, go back to Events Manager and then click Send Test Traffic. This will test if the Facebook Pixel code is working properly. Note however that it may take several minutes to make the update. The status that you will find should say "Active."

The next step after this is to create events for your website. We'll go over that later.

c. The last option is when your site is hosted on a popular web platform or if your site uses a tag manager. Examples of ecommerce platforms and tag managers include Google Tag Manager and Squarespace—they allow you to install Pixel without having to make you doodle with your website's code.

So, how do you install Pixel in this case? Go to Events Manager and then go to the Partner Integrations Tab.

In that section select your tag manager or the platform that hosts your site. After selecting it click on Connect Account. Finally, click on the appropriate settings as you follow the prompts that will come up on screen.

Remember that you will want to click Send Test Traffic after your Facebook Pixel is installed. This will test if Pixel was installed correctly and is functioning. If everything is working well then click **Continue**.

3. Track the Desired Events on Your Dropshipping Site

Now as you can see from the list of events above, not all 17 of the standard ones will directly contribute to conversion. Simply put, not every event of the standard 17 can move a site visitor into an actual buyer.

That is why you need to select whether Pixel will start tracking upon the loading of a page or after a specific action of the visitor has been performed. Here is brief description of these types of actions:

- *Page Load*: this means Pixel will track a visitor with each loading of a web page from your site. This includes completed purchases as well as any form of signing up that the user will perform.
- *Inline Action*: this means Pixel will track any type of action that is done within any specific web page on your site. This will include searches performed, clicks on links on that page, and even a click to the "add to cart" button.

To tell Pixel which events you want to track you just need to toggle each option on or off. You will be shown something like this: (next page)

🔵 Purchase   Show Instructions

⚪ Lead

⚪ Complete Registration

⚪ Add Payment Info

⚪ Add to Cart

🔵 Add to Wishlist   Show Instructions

⚪ Initiate Checkout

⚪ Search

⚪ View Content

⚪ Contact

⚪ Customize Product

⚪ Donate

🔵 Find Location   Show Instructions

Now, what if you want to use your custom events? To do that, go to Custom Conversions within Events Manager. You'll find that on the top left menu. If you haven't created any custom conversion events click on Create Custom Conversion and select the custom rules you want to use.

It would look like this:

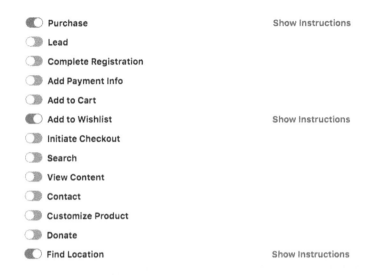

4. Check If Your Setup is Working Using Browser Extensions

We have already shown you one way you can test if your Facebook Pixel setup is working. There is another method that you can use other than actually clicking on a Facebook ad yourself and then buying something.

There is a browser extension called Facebook Pixel Helper. Unfortunately it is only available in Chrome. If you're using Firefox or Edge then you will have to install Chrome first before you can use this little widget.

After installing Pixel Helper on Chrome, go to your dropshipping site that has Facebook Pixel installed on it. When you open that page and if everything is working fine then the "</>" extension icon on the top right will light up and it will turn blue.

This browser extension will basically look for the Pixel code on a page. It will also open a pop up and it will tell you if everything is working properly. If for instance there is something wrong with your setup the pop up will also indicate an error and will give you the appropriate error info so you can correct the problems yourself.

5. Make Sure to Add a Facebook Pixel Notification

Now, this step is more for legality and it is also required by Facebook's terms of use. You see, when you place code on your website that tracks other people's activities that may be considered as a violation of their privacy rights.

There are also other laws that you may be breaking in other countries if you do that. One way to comply with legalities and regulations is to inform your site's visitors that you are collecting their data on your website.

You need to provide a clear notification upfront that you are using Facebook Pixel code on your website. And you should also inform every visitor that their info is being collected through cookies and also by using other methods as well—such as the code used in Pixel.

You've seen these before. You remember those sites that give you that huge warning at the bottom that says their sites uses cookies and such? Yep, you also need to create something like that too.

In order to setup a Pixel Notice on your site, you need to go through the details provided by Section 3: Special Provisions Concerning the Use of Facebook Pixels and SDKs on Facebook's Business Tools terms page, which you can find by visiting https://www.facebook.com/legal/terms/businesstools.

Now, the good news is that Facebook has provided a Cookie Consent Guide that you can use, which you can find here:

https://developers.facebook.com/docs/privacy.

6. First Party and Third Party Cookies

Unless you're in the finance or health business this policy may not apply to you. But it is still good to know. It's more of a legal matter than anything and if you're interested in legalities then you might just want to get at least a heads up about it.

The change happened back in late 2018 when Facebook finally allowed the use of both 1st party as well as 3rd party cookies. If you are advertising your business and you don't want to use 1st party cookies then you now have that option.

This change allowed advertisers and marketers to track data in other browsers such as Firefox and Safari. Note that these browsers have limits on the use of 3rd party cookies. You would usually want to do this if you are in the finance and healthy industry since you're bound by certain privacy laws.

And that is basically how you use Facebook Pixel to retarget previous customers and other potential leads. Pixel also allows you to search for other Facebook users who are likely similar to the users of your site.

It's a better option than to virtually shotgun your ads. With this method you are targeting the right audience with similar interests.

Chapter 10: Growing Your Business to $10,000+ / Month

In the previous chapter we have gone over how you can promote your dropshipping site. I suggest that you start with Facebook first. After you have set that up along with Facebook Pixel, you can wait for your ads to rack up the numbers.

Note that Facebook is the biggest social media channel there is. However, it can be costly. The next place you want to setup your marketing is on Twitter. It is cheaper and you can always start for free.

Finally, you can move on to Instagram and Pinterest maybe after you have seen the numbers and results in either Facebook or Twitter. Check how many conversions you're getting, how much web traffic is generated (how many people visit your site because of your ads), and see how many leads are generated (how many new accounts, add to carts, and checkouts are made).

Check if your market is on Facebook or if it is on Twitter. Remember that these are pay per click methods. You will have to pay these platforms for the amount of traffic they are able to generate on your dropshipping store.

Note that Twitter is seen by many ecommerce marketers as a very reliable social media platform as far as conversion is concerned. According to one study, about 52% of its users tend to buy products that are advertised there. On top of that they have 5 times more customer engagement, which increases your chances of conversion.

This page has a nice info graphic to show you some very interesting numbers:

https://www.webfx.com/blog/social-media/why-twitter-matters-to-marketing-infographic/

However, that doesn't mean that you should forget about Facebook and the other social media channels. Facebook actually reports some pretty good ROI for digital marketers. Consider the following:

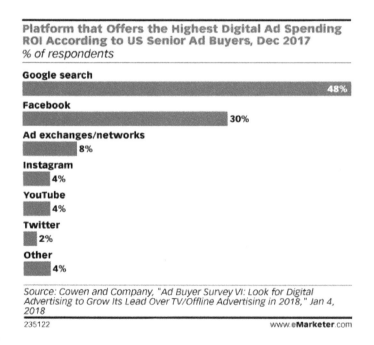

Platform that Offers the Highest Digital Ad Spending ROI According to US Senior Ad Buyers, Dec 2017
% of respondents

- Google search — 48%
- Facebook — 30%
- Ad exchanges/networks — 8%
- Instagram — 4%
- YouTube — 4%
- Twitter — 2%
- Other — 4%

Source: Cowen and Company, "Ad Buyer Survey VI: Look for Digital Advertising to Grow Its Lead Over TV/Offline Advertising in 2018," Jan 4, 2018

235122   www.eMarketer.com

Scaling Your Business

Scaling your business means that you need to move forward and grow. At first you will be a one man team. If you can manage that then it will be great to do it by yourself. There won't be that many tasks to do at first.

All you need to do is to create your customer personas, do your research, setup your dropshipping site (or some other sales channel described in an earlier chapter), register your business (i.e. sole proprietorship at first), pick and post your products, advertise in your selected medium, and then watch the analytics.

You need to determine where your customers are actually coming from. That will take a while. You will also need to craft ad campaigns, which means creating images, videos, slogans, and what not.

To scale your business you need to do the following:

- Add complimentary products
- Use the power of email lists
- Increase your market spend
- Hire a virtual assistant (you can't do it all your own anymore)
- Go multichannel

Add Complimentary Products

Find out which of your listed products sell. You will then go back to Amazon or some other online retailing portal (like eBay for instance or a competing dropshipping site).

Look for your product there. You're not the only one selling it, remember? If you're product is unique then you should look for similar product. For instance, if you're selling waterproof Bluetooth speakers, then look for Bluetooth speakers that are also waterproof and are about the same price.

And then look at the "People who viewed this item also viewed" part of those product pages. Another section is the "often bought together" section that shows which other products were also bought with that Bluetooth speaker.

That will give you a good idea of the complimentary products that you can sell on your site as well.

You can also brainstorm things too. Think of other possible products that will complement your product. If you're selling a Vitamin D supplement, your customers might also be interested in Calcium and Magnesium supplements as well.

Why? Well, you need a balance of all of these three nutrients so that you can get the most of the benefits you get from all of them. Do your due diligence—do some research.

You can also just create a different offer—a competing product perhaps. And then see if people buy that instead or just head off to their own choice of complimentary product. The goal is to make people make their move and observe how what they do on your website. Make use of the analytics tools provided to you from the different social media channels and Google as well.

You're Going to Get Busy with the Problems

Here's a bit of fair warning. As your sales increase expect to get more returns and customer complaints. **Big Hint**: deal with it as fast as you can and as efficiently as you can or else your reputation will suffer.

Returns

Customers will return products for one reason or another. You should immediately check the return policy on that product (30 day or 45 day money back guarantees etc.). Base your next move on that policy provided by your supplier.

Chargebacks

Sometimes you will get chargeback notifs. More often than not a chargeback is actually fraudulent. However, the bank won't give you a lot of time so you better act quickly. You need to provide proof that you actually delivered the goods.

Evidence come in the form of packing slip, tracking information, and the exact order that was made.

Shipping Type

Most dropshippers will offer free shipping and just work the cost into the list price they display on their online store. How are they able to do that? Well, they opt for flat rate shipping. It's the same charge for all items you sell.

But that is not always available. Sometimes you will have to use per type rates especially if the item being shipped is heavier or larger. If you're shipping larger packages your best carrier options are FedEx and UPS. They give better rates.

If you are usually shipping smaller items then USPS is the go to carrier. They can charge less than $5 per package.

Customer Support

Expect to do some customer support yourself at certain times. A lot of dropshippers use support software to help them manage customer complaints and provide support options. Here are the top 3 choices for many dropshippers:

- Desk (operated by Salesforce)
- Help Scout (go to option for personalized service and it has a pretty good support ticket system)

- Zendesk (has lots of pricing options—great for beginners with smaller budgets).

Email Lists

Email lists are still a staple for ecommerce. If you already have your own website and your own dropshipping site then it makes sense to create an email list. You can offer discount coupon codes, product guides, brochures, create discount events or anything that you can provide for free in exchange for your customer's email address.

You should also indicate that you will be sending them promotional items on their emails when you ask for their email addresses.

You also shouldn't pepper your subscribers with emails every day. That will be annoying. You should schedule your emails like maybe once or twice a week. Email them whenever you have a sale coming up.

Here are some of the types of emails that you might want to send your customers:

- Welcome email
- Help email
- Answers to inquiries
- Unexpected freebie email
- Newsletters
- Important events email

You will want to use an email marketing service later on. It's easy to send out those emails to 25 or even 50 of your close friends and relatives. But as your customer base grows and as your website gains popularity, expect your list of emails to grow to the hundreds (or even thousands).

That is why you need the help of an email marketing service to help manage all of that. Mailchimp is the popular email marketing brand out there. However, there are other alternatives such as Benchmark, MailerLite, GetResponse, and others. Check out their rates and see which ones fit your budget.

You will also want to spend time to learn more about email marketing. Again it's a huge subject and it can't be covered comprehensively in this book.

Increase Your Marketing Spend

After a lot of fine tuning (i.e. mistakes and blunders) you will find out the best practices and the best products for your dropshipping store. You will then need to increase your marketing spend.

That means increasing your marketing budget. You already know your niche and your market. Now it's time to get more sales and in order to do that you need more aggressive marketing ergo more funds spent on ads and analytics monitoring.

Hiring a Virtual Assistant

As your success grows your market grows. That also means you will get more customer complaints and experience more problems. You will end up getting so busy it can drive you crazy.

That means you have grown your business to a point where you can't do it on your own anymore. Then you have to delegate some of the repetitive tasks of your business to someone else and focus on the important stuff—marketing, sales, and advertising.

This is where a virtual assistant can come into play. Alternatively you can hire someone in the neighborhood but that might entail some legalities which can drain more of your funds. Maybe you can do that later when your business has grown a little bit bigger.

For now a virtual assistant who will work part time will have to do. You can delegate the following tasks to a VA:

- Graphic design
- SEO work
- Website maintenance
- Creating blog posts
- Writing newsletters
- Updating inventory
- Processing invoices
- Social media management
- Customer service

So, where do you hire your prospective VA? There are lots of platforms where Vas post their professional profiles. You can hire them from Upwork, Zirtual, or Freelancer. Those are the top 3 nowadays but there are others too.

 Note that sooner or later you will need to assemble a team or several teams. Some VAs and in house employees will be in charge of marketing. Some will be tasked with customer service (you'll need help dealing with hundreds if not thousands of customers), and others will be tasked with site management, product research, and other tasks as well.

Conclusion

Just like many would-be entrepreneurs out there the main reason why they fail is because they failed to try.

Dropshipping isn't easy. It's not a get rich quick scheme. The ROI can be dismal at times. But if you work at it and set things up right then you are creating a huge source of passive income.

You will be doing 100% of the work at first. But as the business grows the more tasks you will delegate to your employees. Is it scary? Of course it is. It's a tough environment but it is a sustainable one.

Remember it is projected to grow exponentially in the next few years. Do you want to just sit back and watch the action or take part and take off into the future?

It's all up to you.

I hope that the information here has helped you get the gist of the huge work ahead in case you decide to engage in dropshipping.

To your success!

Thank you

Before you go, I just wanted to say thank you for purchasing my book.

You could have picked from dozens of other books on the same topic but you took a chance and chose this one.

So, a HUGE thanks to you for getting this book and for reading all the way to the end.

Now I wanted to ask you for a small favor. ***Could you please consider posting a review on the platform? Reviews are one of the easiest ways to support the work of independent authors.***

This feedback will help me continue to write the type of books that will help you get the results you want. So if you enjoyed it, please let me know!

Lastly, don't forget to grab a copy of your Free Bonuses ***"The Fastest Way to Make Money with Affiliate Marketing"*** and ***"Top 10 Affiliate Offers to Promote"***

Just go to the link below.

https://theartofmastery.com/chandler-free-gift

Milton Keynes UK
Ingram Content Group UK Ltd.
UKHW020629151124
2865UKWH00032B/236